The Last Wife

the
LAST
WIFE
Kate Hennig

**PLAYWRIGHTS
CANADA PRESS**
Toronto

The Last Wife © 2015 by Kate Hennig

For professional or amateur production rights, please contact:
The Gary Goddard Agency
149 Church Street, 2nd Floor
Toronto, ON M5B 1Y4
416-928-0299, meaghan@garygoddardagency.com

LIBRARY AND ARCHIVES CANADA CATALOGUING IN PUBLICATION
Hennig, Kate, author
        The last wife / Kate Hennig. -- First edition.

Issued in print and electronic formats.
ISBN 978-1-77091-410-0 (paperback).--ISBN 978-1-77091-411-7 (pdf).--ISBN 978-1-77091-412-4 (epub).--ISBN 978-1-77091-413-1 (mobi)

        1. Henry VIII, King of England, 1491-1547--Drama. 2. Catharine Parr, Queen, consort of Henry VIII, King of England, 1512-1548--Drama. .I. Title.

PS8615.E543L37 2015   C812'.6   C2015-904058-2
                                             C2015-904059-0

We acknowledge the financial support of the Canada Council for the Arts, the Ontario Arts Council (OAC), the Ontario Media Development Corporation, and the Government of Canada through the Canada Book Fund for our publishing activities. Nous remercions l'appui financier du Conseil des Arts du Canada, le Conseil arts de l'Ontario (CAO), la Société de développement de l'industrie des médias de l'Ontario, et le Gouvernement du Canada par l'entremise du Fonds du livre du Canada pour nos activités d'édition.

 Canada Council Conseil des arts
for the Arts   du Canada

 ONTARIO ARTS COUNCIL
CONSEIL DES ARTS DE L'ONTARIO
an Ontario government agency
un organisme du gouvernement de l'Ontario

 Canadä

 Ontario
Ontario Media Development
Corporation

To my parents and siblings, for the contributions that only parents and siblings can make, and to Andy McKim: caring and supportive co-parent of my literary children.

The Last Wife is an *imagining* of history. Oh yes, it's based on actual people and events, and while portions of it are deliciously accurate, some bits may offend the historically precise among you, while still others are completely and utterly fabricated. My priority in choosing must always favour the dramatic.

What I am deeply interested in is the humanity of these iconic historical characters. I want to imagine what makes them do what they do, just as I want to imagine what makes Margaret Thatcher, Indira Gandhi, and Aung San Suu Kyi do what they do. They are human after all. They have mothers, fathers, siblings, and children. One expects that they play tennis, watch television, read books; they laugh, worry, drink too much coffee from time to time. It fascinates me to create these personal possibilities and then imagine how they might lead to some of the major decisions that history records. It helps us to see women as a moving political force of history away from the battlefields and the halls of office. It helps us see the Tudor wave of feminism.

—KH

The Last Wife was first produced by the Stratford Festival and premiered at the Studio Theatre in Stratford, Ontario, on August 14, 2015, with the following cast and creative team:

Kate: Maev Beaty
Thom: Gareth Potter
Henry: Joseph Ziegler
Mary: Sara Farb
Bess: Bahia Watson
Eddie: Jonah Q. Gribble

Artistic director: Antoni Cimolino
Executive director: Anita Gaffney
Producer: David Auster
Casting director: Beth Russell
Creative planning director: Jason Miller

Director: Alan Dilworth
Designer: Yannick Larivee
Assistant designer: Nancy Anne Perrin
Lighting designer: Kimberly Purtell
Assistant lighting designer: Kaileigh Krysztofiak
Dramaturge: Bob White
Original dramaturge: Andy McKim
Sound designer: Alexander MacSween
Stage manager: Melissa Rood
Assistant stage manager: Katherine Arcus
Production assistant: Jacki Brabazon
Production stage managers: Bona Duncan and Marylu Moyer
Technical director: Robbin Cheesman

PLAYWRIGHT'S NOTES

This is a contemporary play. This is a domestic play. No historical costuming or accents are required. Diversity in casting is strongly encouraged.

The following edited versions of extant manuscripts appear in the script: two letters of Edward VI; the marriage vows of Henry VIII and Katherine Parr; *The Confession of Lady Mary*; *The Third Act of Succession*; the resolution for and commission of Katherine Parr's regency by Henry VIII; *The Prayer of Queen Esther for Help Against Her Enemies* and *The Prayer of Manasses, Sixth King of Judah* from Katherine Parr's "Personal Prayerbook"; the lyrics of "Whoso That Will All Feats Obtain" by Henry VIII; sections of John Foxe's *Acts and Monuments*; and an epitaph by John Parkhurst.

Word / word indicates the next speaker should overlap their dialogue at the slash, including at the beginning of a line.

There's something deeply, mercilessly wrong in the way the world treats women. Gender equality is the single most important struggle on the planet. Patriarchy is a crime against humanity.

—Stephen Lewis
Stratford Festival Forum
August 17, 2013

CHARACTERS

Kate: a lady of the court, later a queen; early thirties
Bess: a princess; eleven to fourteen years old
Mary: a princess; late twenties
Henry: a king; in his fifties
Thom: a naval officer; late thirties
Eddie: a prince; six to nine years old

ACT ONE
SCENE ONE: MEETING

In public. KATE *is wearing a grey gown, with seventeen little buttons of gold garnished with small pearls.* THOM *stands across from her.*

KATE   It's a bit surprising to me, that's all.

THOM   What is?

KATE   The way you know me.

THOM   Not enough of you.

KATE   You see through me.

THOM   In what way?

KATE   Well what am I feeling?

THOM   Guilt.

KATE   In that way.

THOM   I wish you didn't.

KATE   If anything's true it's what we feel.

THOM   So you feel guilty.

KATE	My husband is very good to me.
THOM	Not for much longer.
KATE	Who knows.
THOM	The doctor.
KATE	The doctor said he wouldn't make it through the trip up north last year.

THOM touches KATE's shoulder.

THOM	I'm not suggesting you don't love John.
KATE	I've been devoted to John.
THOM	But he doesn't give you what you need.
KATE	He gives me what's his to give. That's all I can ask.
THOM	It's all I ask of you. But it doesn't stop my desire. Or yours, I hope.

THOM drops one of the straps on KATE's gown.

| KATE | It's almost dinner. |
| THOM | He's always late. |

KATE stops his hand.

/ Sorry.

KATE	Sorry.
THOM	That's okay. I'm patient.
KATE	You are.
THOM	Sure. It's pretty rare.
KATE	What is?
THOM	Your self-control, considering . . .
KATE	What?
THOM	Well, how much fun can it be with John? What is he, seventy?

KATE	Forty-nine.
THOM	Still . . .
KATE	He gives me other things: stability, loyalty.
THOM	He can't protect you.
KATE	He can. He does.
THOM	Except . . . ?
KATE	Only that once.
THOM	Once was enough.
KATE	He shares his children with me. There's more to life you know than sexual—
THOM	Pleasure?
KATE	Achievement.
THOM	But if you've never even known the fun you / can
KATE	It makes me uncomfortable to talk about it.
THOM	Okay.

He looks at her.

KATE	What.
THOM	I'm imagining you . . . with me . . .
KATE	You're embarrassing / me
THOM	having fun . . .
KATE	Please . . .

He touches her face.

THOM	I won't let anyone hurt you.
KATE	That's a lot to promise.

HENRY enters the room.

HENRY   Thom!

THOM   I— / oh . . .

HENRY   I forgot you were coming.

(to KATE) Hi.

(to THOM, but not taking his gaze from KATE) An introduction to the lovely lady, if you will.

THOM   Uhhvv course, His Majesty, Henry the Eighth, by the grace of God, King of England and France: Defender of the Faith, and on earth, immediately under Christ, Supreme Head of the Church of England.

HENRY   Don't forget Ireland. *Never* forget Ireland.

And . . . ? Thomas . . . ?

THOM   Majesty?

HENRY gestures toward KATE.

Uhh, sorry . . . I . . . Katherine Parr, Majesty. The Lady Latimer. Wife to John Neville, the third Baron Latimer.

KATE   Majesty.

HENRY   And the ever-handsome playboy Thom Seymour . . . Darn! No title.

(to KATE) Come from the North, haven't you? I knew your father.

HENRY formally kisses KATE on the lips.

Katherine Parr.

Too many Katherines, don't you think. Too many Marys. Too many Henrys, for that matter. What is it with the English and their names. Only the half-dozen we can spell correctly, I suppose.

Lady Latimer: your husband is not with us I see. A miraculous recovery is not expected?

KATE	He sends his best wishes, Majesty.
HENRY	Does he. Wants to placate me with his "best wishes"? Thinks that "best wishes" will deter me from avenging his sedition? from wiping out the estates he pilfered from me?
KATE	I'm afraid I'm little equipped to understand the intricacies of my husband's estates, or your intentions for them.
HENRY	Is that so.
KATE	If you'll be so generous, Majesty, as to spell out your plan, I'm sure I'll be in your debt.
HENRY	Oh, you'll be in my debt all right. When he croaks? Accounts must be settled. Even you must be equipped to grasp that much.
	(to THOM) Didn't take you too long to get chummy with the Lady Latimer, eh, Thom? Providing her a little sturdy comfort as her old man flails listlessly toward his end?
THOM	We enjoy taking the air together, Majesty.
HENRY	Quite. And what other little gems do you share, along with particles of oxygen, heh?
THOM	Well . . . we've been discussing Plato's *Republic*. You see, we're / both
HENRY	Whoa. Thomas. *You're* reading Plato?
THOM	Lady Latimer suggested I read / it and
HENRY	Ah hah! An ill-equipped mind, has she? Yet reads the classics, and all. Does she have a little French? a little Italian, perhaps? In what language is the lady studying Plato, one might ask. For the sake of . . . conversation.
KATE	In Latin, Your Majesty.
HENRY	Pah.

(in Latin) Quando mortuus fuerit vir tuus? [When will your husband die?]

KATE   (in Latin) Doctores dicunt finita septimana. [The doctors say within the week.]

HENRY   (in Italian) Ti manca la tua casa nel Nord? [Do you miss your home in the North?]

KATE   (in Italian) Solo a Natale. [Only at Christmas.]

HENRY   (in French) Et la cour? Ça vous amuse? [And court? Does it amuse you?]

KATE   (in French) Je n'ai guère besoin de divertissement, Majesté. Je suis ici pour servir. [I have little need for amusement, Majesty. I am here to serve.]

HENRY   (in Spanish) Déjame imaginar alguna forma agradable en el que usted me padria servir. [Let me imagine some enjoyable ways in which you could serve me.]

KATE   You have me there, Majesty.

HENRY   What?! No Spanish? Thomas. Translate for your Platonic friend.

THOM   His Majesty said he'd be happy for you to serve him.

HENRY   No. I said, I'd like to imagine the ways *in which* you could serve me. A very different connotation there, my brother.

THOM says nothing. HENRY looks directly at him.

(*back to* KATE) Did you tell him about the necklace I gave you?

THOM looks at KATE. KATE *looks at* THOM, *then quickly back at* HENRY.

Well, that might be a nice little going-away confab for the two of you.

(*with new energy*) Thomas:

THOM	Majesty.
HENRY	Ever foraged in the Low Countries?
THOM	Majesty?
HENRY	Tsk, tsk, tsk. Ever been to Holland, I meant. Mind up. Mind up.
THOM	Yes, Majesty.
HENRY	Enjoy it?
THOM	They're a good people, I think, the Dutch.
HENRY	A dull people, I think, the Dutch. What *use* are they to me, eh, Thom?
THOM	Dependable allies; strategic location. Of course their allegiance can waver from time to / time
HENRY	Perfect. You will now have the opportunity to affirm the loyalty of Holland and assert the continuing necessity of diplomacy with our Crown.
THOM	You're sending me / to . . . ?
HENRY	You'll report back to me quarterly at Council.

THOM is halted.

THOM	Pardon me?
HENRY	*(to KATE)* Did I not make myself clear?
THOM	Reporting to Council, yes. Me, / sir.
HENRY	Quarterly. That's every three months. And if you behave really well on your boat you may finally earn yourself that elusive little title: how does Lord High Admiral sound?
THOM	Extremely flattering, my lord.
HENRY	Might win some points in your family feud, eh?
THOM	/ But

HENRY	*(aside to* KATE*)* Like greyhounds, that Seymour clan. And my ass is the rabbit.
	Have fun with the dikes, Thom. Prepare to leave within the month.
THOM	Yes, but Kate and I—
	THOM hesitates. HENRY *lets him sit in it.*
HENRY	Thomas?
THOM	No.
HENRY	Kate what? *This* Kate? What of her?
THOM	I . . . Within the month, Majesty.
HENRY	Arrangements will be made for your reception in Amsterdam. Let's hope the Dutch weren't too offended by the huge fuck-up I made with that girl from Cleves. She had none, by the way. Teutonic women . . . they all look like heifers.
	I have no doubt the ditch-sitters will be delighted by your impeccable style and refinement. Especially that beard, Thomas. That's gotta hold sway with the ladies.
	Right. Off to the dining room. A handsome bugger like you, I'm sure Mary would love to get her hooks in before you set sail.
	Lady Latimer and I will follow shortly.
THOM	Majesty.
HENRY	Toodle-oo.
	THOM goes. A silence.
	(sighing) Okay then . . .
	Lady Latimer.
KATE	Katherine.
HENRY	Oh, that name: can we please distinguish you in some way?

KATE	You, you might call me . . . Parr.
HENRY	A tad military, don't you think.

> HENRY *checks* KATE *out.*

You afraid of me? Parr?

KATE	Wary.
HENRY	Wise. I get what I want.
KATE	A privilege you've earned.
HENRY	A privilege I was born to.
KATE	And you want something from me?
HENRY	*(a fact)* I've reached an impasse, you see: no one wants to introduce me to their daughters anymore. There may be a dozen witnesses standing behind the doctor while the girl spreads her legs but if I say she isn't a virgin, she isn't a virgin. Proof will somehow be provided and they all die: the virgin, the witnesses, the family. Even the good doctor.
KATE	You have authority.
HENRY	I do.
KATE	And wield it.
HENRY	Can't fight battles anymore. I resort to other sport.
KATE	Some might call that brutality.
HENRY	But not anyone here: am I right?
KATE	You're always right.
HENRY	I've been doing my homework. When it comes to husbands . . . you've not been very lucky.
KATE	I've been well provided for.

HENRY	Right, but John's gonna bite the dust pretty soon and then where'll you be. I can certainly provide a better future than you'll get fooling around with Thomas.
KATE	Thomas and I—
HENRY	Yes?
KATE	We . . . have an understanding.
HENRY	Someday you'll tell me all about it.
	I sent a gift. You accepted it.
KATE	The men who brought it didn't seem to want to take it back.
HENRY	Which necklace did they bring?
KATE	Sapphire, with a ruby and pearl drop. I believe you first gave it to Jane.
HENRY	Who told you that?
KATE	She's wearing it in one of her portraits.
HENRY	*(precisely)* You will not speak of Jane.

A moment.

	Does it suit you? The necklace?
KATE	Did it suit Jane?

This lands.

HENRY	A frisky little filly. I'll send you another. And when your darling husband kicks off, I'll have some fancy mourning clothes made for you. Something cinched at the waist that shows off your rack.

HENRY looks at KATE again.

	When he dies, I want your answer.
KATE	I have a choice?
HENRY	They've all had a choice.

HENRY heads off, leaving KATE alone.

(as he leaves) Hey Thom. You can ask her about the necklace now.

THOM carefully re-enters.

(from off) And don't forget to wash your hands before dinner.

THOM   I can't believe you! What were you thinking?!

KATE   The KING gave me a necklace! What could I do?!

THOM   You could've told me!

KATE   How would that help?

THOM   I would have stopped you coming here!

KATE   You think I could have prevented this?!

THOM   Damn him! He always gets what he wants.

Their heads start to spin.

KATE   What do I do? What am I supposed to *do*?!

THOM   He's the king: you marry him.

KATE   Marry the—? No. Aren't there options?

THOM   Look! I can't think right now! He's sending me to Holland!

KATE   But you and I *have* something, / and

THOM   I know

KATE   and I'm just feeling safe with / you

THOM   and you / should

KATE   and starting to feel more / than

THOM   that's what I want / but

KATE   and

THOM   there's nothing either of us can do!

KATE	The king's wife.
	Me.
	A moment.
	I want to marry *you*.
	A moment.
	KATE throws herself on THOM, *kissing him. It's a clumsy, chaotic attempt, you know, when teeth bang together.* THOM *manoeuvres this into something luscious and sexy.*
	KATE pushes back from THOM, *excited. Then she makes a decision.*
KATE	You're reporting to Council every three months . . .
	THOM *registers this.*
THOM	No, no, no: he'd kill us.
KATE	Not for this. It's only a promise. Of something to come.
THOM	That's a mighty long tease.
KATE	A diversion. From our mutual . . . exile. Do you think?
THOM	There'll be plenty of girls to divert with in Holland.
KATE	I know.
THOM	And you'll be sleeping with Henry.
KATE	Yes.
THOM	And we'll . . . ?
KATE	Have this secret thing.
THOM	Dangerous thing.
KATE	Exactly. Dangerous.
	THOM *capitulates.*
THOM	You know how easy it is for me to be with most women?

KATE	But is it just a little thrilling that it's hard to be with me?
THOM	It scares me. C'mere.
KATE	We have to go in to dinner.
THOM	It starts now?
KATE	When you touch me I lose my brain. And I need my brain.

SCENE TWO: RESPECT*

In private. HENRY is writing. MARY enters with a book. HENRY looks up.

HENRY	Mistress Mary, quite contrary, how does your garden grow?
MARY	What—should I play your sweet little daughter again and finish your rhyme?
HENRY	Did you find it?
MARY	Beside her bed.
HENRY	And you can put it back there?
MARY	Whatcha gonna give me?
HENRY	A wink. Maybe a nod.
MARY	Some deal.

MARY hands HENRY the book.

What do you want it for?

HENRY	I wrote her a poem, and I want her to find it.
MARY	You darn romantic, you.
HENRY	She needs encouraging. Think it'll work?

---

* The title of the poem Henry VIII wrote in a book of Katherine Parr's.

MARY	I'm not much for your poetry.
HENRY	Everybody's a critic. I'm gonna write it in the margin.

HENRY starts to write.

MARY	You really like Kate?

HENRY looks up, shrugs his shoulders.

HENRY	What's not to like?

SCENE THREE: COURTSHIP

At table. HENRY is at his desk. KATE is dressed in black—something cinched at the waist that shows off her rack—and carrying a briefcase.

KATE	I've thought about it a lot. I want to assure you of that.
HENRY	Good.
KATE	And I'd like to offer a counter proposal.
HENRY	I see.

KATE sets her briefcase on the table.

KATE	I'd rather be your mistress.

HENRY laughs.

You said I had a choice.

HENRY	Not that choice.
KATE	Taking your record into consideration, mistress is the better bargain.
HENRY	Yeah, but I can't get it up for mistresses anymore. Some weird connubial necessity in my conscience.
KATE	I assumed you had more liberal tendencies.

HENRY   I'm capricious. That makes me a fascist, not a liberal.

KATE   In that case . . . I'll entertain your "proposal" as a business venture: all expectations above board and in writing.

Something starts brewing in HENRY.

HENRY   Uhuh. Strictly business.

KATE opens her briefcase. She takes out files and ledgers.

KATE   I've drawn up an inventory of my current holdings. You can have your lawyers look it over, but I believe you'll find it accurate and complete: *(a file)* here, the estates from my previous husbands; *(a file)* clear descriptions of the jewellery my mother left me—which must, and *will* be returned to me upon your passing; *(a ledger)* these are rents from my tenanted properties; *(a ledger)* all current accounts itemized and audited. From you I'll need lists of the jointure you intend; I prefer to choose my own properties—I found this best in my previous cohabitation agreements; I have particular tastes in jewellery and ask that I might select from jewels and garments belonging to the state, rather than having them assigned; all other prov/isions

HENRY grabs KATE by the arm.

HENRY   Were you raped at your home / in the North?

KATE   Don't you / touch me

HENRY   —when the rebels garrisoned the castle? Did you miscarry that baby? Or did you abort it yourself.

KATE struggles to free herself from his grasp. HENRY holds her fast.

KATE   You are unbelievable.

HENRY   I've got the dirt on everyone, so don't think you have the upper hand just cuz I've got the hots for you. You don't tell me how things are done, get it?! I do as I please. I'm like a child in that way, Parr. Don't you want a child to love? A barren woman like you?

KATE   I wouldn't love you if you paid me.

KATE kicks HENRY in the leg. He lets go.

HENRY   AAAARRRRGH! NOT THE / LEG!

KATE   You don't grab / me like that!

HENRY   That's treason, you little—! Assaulting the / king?

KATE   Then have / me arrested!

HENRY   I should have you— Aaaaah, you don't know how / much that—damn you—

KATE   Go on! Have me / arrested! Or I'll do it again!

HENRY   I'm not having you arrested, so you can stop with the— Holy crap! I see stars. Look. Stars.

KATE stands in horror of her own actions. Once HENRY can breathe again:

Forget your petty account books: *that's* what you bring. Wow. Just a little intractability.

Marry me, okay? Come on. I need someone like you: I need a woman who can survive me—like you survived those rebels who took advantage of you—who can study my little Council of Crocodiles, and walk across their backs to the other side.

I need a woman to educate my son. To be a mother to him. And if you can have another son while you're at it, that'll be the butter. I'll make it worth your while: the flower budget alone!

What? do you want to love a pansy like Seymour? Cuz he's cute? with his beard, and his buff body? Cuz you and he can stroll sedately through the gardens at Hampton and exchange clever ideas about fucking Plato?

The blood drains from KATE's face.

Parr . . . ?

KATE He's civil.

HENRY And I'm a creep. But at least a dying creep. You have a reputation for being good with dying husbands.

KATE *(wobbly)* I can't quite . . . breathe . . .

HENRY gets KATE a chair.

HENRY Here. Sit. Water?

KATE Please.

HENRY pours KATE a glass; she drinks.

I'm suddenly . . . a bit dizzy.

HENRY It happens to the best of them.

Listen: I'll give you anything you ask if you'll see my son on that throne when I die.

KATE There's no way of guaran—

Look. I'll do my best.

KATE considers.

I'll do my best.

HENRY I respect that.

KATE You do?

HENRY Sure. I respect your honesty.

KATE You respect my honesty, but at the same time you can kill me with the stroke of a pen.

HENRY I'm pretty sure I can still do it with the stroke of a sword. But then I wouldn't get what I want, would I: my son . . . on the throne. That's my priority. And yours. Clear?

	A moment.
KATE	Clear.
	A moment.
	Wait. I have one rule.
HENRY	You have. A rule.
KATE	Regarding our . . . conjugal relationship . . .
HENRY	Yyyyes?
KATE	In the bedroom I have / to . . .
HENRY	Yyyyes?
KATE	I have to . . . lead.
HENRY	Men like that.
KATE	I mean, it's up to me whether we . . .
HENRY	Wait, wait, wait: you want me to ask you before . . . ?
KATE	Yes. I do.
HENRY	Ohh, because / of
KATE	Because I was raped. Yes. And you will never use that information to control me again. Practise the stroke of your sword if you like, but I won't do anything I don't choose to do. Not in that department.
HENRY	Clear.
	KATE is thrown off by this.
KATE	You can agree to that?
HENRY	We all have our demons.
	A moment.
KATE	Then we have a deal.
	HENRY, rather painfully, gets down on one knee.

HENRY   Katherine. Parr. Will you grant me the great distinction of accepting me as your husband?

KATE is thrown off by this, too.

KATE   I will.

HENRY   That makes me very happy.

HENRY stands.

Well! That sure got the blood going!

He turns to go, then:

Oh hey, I almost forgot. I should give you something.

KATE   Give me?

HENRY   A gift. For our wedding.

KATE   I can't accept a gift before your lawyers sign off.

HENRY   Sheesh, honey, I'm trying to be generous.

KATE   What you can give me is a fair contract.

HENRY   Okay, look: you educate my son—the future King Edward the Sixth—let's say that's your . . . contribution. What can I offer you in exchange?

A moment.

KATE   Where's your daughter?

HENRY   Pulling legs off a spider?

KATE   Not Mary.

Elizabeth.

HENRY   Her! Ha. At Hatfield, where she belongs.

KATE   Give me Bess.

HENRY   What do you mean: "Give me Bess"?

KATE   As part of this household. Bring her back.

HENRY	Born of a whore, that girl.
KATE	I'll teach Edward for you but let me educate Bess alongside him.
HENRY	A toy? In exchange for a prince? Not much of a bargain.
KATE	Call it a gift. You can even call it generosity.
HENRY	Bess it is.

KATE contemplates her success and takes her packed briefcase off the table.

SCENE FOUR: A NEW MOTHER

At table. BESS is embroidering.

BESS	*(speaking to KATE, who is offstage)* It's a long time since I was here. To stay, I mean. I always kind of hated it here. Nothing to do, no one to spend time with. When I told my friends I was coming they were all, "Weddings are boring: they play stupid music, and old people dance holding on to each other." But I'm . . . a little bit excited, aren't you? Do you like my new dress? I want to wear a real wedding dress one day. White. With lace, and frills. Ooooo, and pearl buttons. Mary doesn't want to get married. She thinks men are stupid. Do you know how many engagements she's had?
KATE	*(from off)* I can imagine.
BESS	I lost count at twelve. The first time she was two years old. How can anyone get married at two years old? That's weird.
KATE	*(from off)* Marriages happen at different times in our lives and for all sorts of reasons.
BESS	How many reasons can there be for a two-year-old?

KATE enters in a simple, elegant dress, carrying a folder. She has her jewellery in her hand and places it on the table.

Oh. Your dress is so plain.

KATE opens the folder and sits to write.

What is that you're writing?

KATE   A letter to your brother. About school.

BESS   Don't we have to go in a minute?

KATE   Your father has a rather strict time frame regarding Eddie's education.

BESS   Are you his teacher now?

KATE   I'm in charge of his teachers.

BESS   Because you're going to be queen?

KATE   That's my new job.

BESS   Being my mother is part of that job, too.

KATE   It is.

BESS   Do you want to be my mother?

KATE   I think I do.

BESS   Do you want to be queen?

KATE   In a way.

BESS   Did you dream of it when you were a little girl?

KATE   Always.

BESS is surprised by this.

BESS   You did?! Did you love the dresses?

KATE   The amazing dresses.

BESS   Cloth of gold brocade. That's my favourite.

KATE   I dreamt of what I might be able to do. If I was queen.

BESS   Yeah. And now you are.

KATE   Imagine.

            A moment.

BESS   I dream of it, too.

KATE   You have that right.

BESS   I dream I get my way a lot.

KATE   Ha hah! We have that in common.

BESS   It's not really fair, is it. Eddie's the youngest, but he's a boy, so he gets to be king. Mary and I . . . well, Father decided we're officially bastards.

KATE   He shouldn't use that word.

BESS   He won't let us be called Princess. I am to be called "The King's Daughter, Lady Elizabeth" instead.

KATE   You'd like to be called Princess.

BESS   It is shorter. Father loves Eddie. So he's called Prince.

            A moment.

            Do you love my father?

            A moment.

KATE   Did he love your mother?

BESS   *(a fact)* He had her head cut off.

KATE   Right.

BESS   I wasn't even three.

            She had a purple velvet dress. It was left to me.

KATE   Did your father love Jane?

BESS   Do you think that's why he loves Eddie? Because he loved Jane?

Hey! Do you know Jane's brother Thom? All the girls at Hatfield think he's soooo cute. And what a great dancer. Jane . . . was pretty, I guess.

But you know what? *(a secret)* She didn't *read*, at least not for fun. Don't you think that's weird? She . . . can't have been very smart.

Father and Jane . . . They'd sit in the living room and embroider.

KATE   Embroider?

BESS   *(showing her embroidery)* Father likes needlepoint. He likes to ride on a horse and stick people through with a lance and then afterwards he likes to sit by the fire with a canvas and a skein of silk.

> *KATE begins to put her jewellery on.*

KATE   You know, Bess, my mother didn't teach me embroidery.

BESS   *(of KATE's bracelet)* Here: let me.

She didn't?

KATE   I never could do bracelets by myself.

She taught me Aristotle. And Euripides, and Plutarch. She said that's a strong foundation for a girl's advancement.

Hnh.

I'll teach them to you. You're a clever girl.

Things need to change around this place.

BESS   Like what?

KATE   Girls doing needlepoint, for starters. And your father needs to learn that a girl who was born a princess has the right to be called a princess.

BESS   I'd like that. But I don't know about teaching Father. He'll see what you're doing. He's pretty smart, you know.

KATE   Oh, I know. But . . . *(a secret)* when I was a little girl? I dreamt of what this country could be with two smart people running it.

BESS stands gaping at KATE.

SCENE FIVE: A NOTARY'S WITNESS OF THE MARRIAGE OF HENRY VIII AND KATHERINE PARR

In public. A wedding. MARY, BESS, and EDDIE are witnesses. KATE and HENRY read the vows.

HENRY   I, Henry, take thee, Katherine, to my wedded wife, to have and hold, from this day forward: for better, for worse, for richer, for poorer, in sickness and in health, till death us do part. And thereto I plight unto thee my troth.

KATE   I, Katherine, take thee, Henry, to my wedded husband: to have and to hold, from this day forward: for better, for worse, for richer, for poorer, in sickness, and in health, to be cour—

KATE stops as she realizes what she has to say.

HENRY   *(prompting)* . . . to be courteous and compliant in bed and / at . . .

MARY laughs.

KATE   This is not—

HENRY looks KATE in the eye. She co-operates.

To be courteous and compliant in bed and at board, till death us do part. And thereto I plight unto thee my troth.

HENRY places a ring on KATE's finger.

HENRY With this ring, I thee wed. And with my body I thee worship; and with all my worldly goods I thee honour.

HENRY kisses KATE on the cheek. He looks around at the congregation.

(with a cheerful face) Yay!

SCENE SIX: WOUND

At bed. KATE and HENRY. There is a basin of water nearby.

KATE That was unfair. To sneak that into the vow.

HENRY Your disapproval is noted.

KATE We had an agreement. About the bed part.

HENRY Things have to have a certain sheen. Don't worry, I've accepted your terms.

A moment.

KATE Let me see the leg.

HENRY No.

KATE We'll both have to get naked at some point, I'm guessing. Let me see it.

HENRY You can smell it from there.

KATE Everyone can smell it.

HENRY Not me. Not anymore.

HENRY reveals the leg. KATE takes in the sight.

KATE They've been cutting it.

HENRY To drain the pus.

KATE	Does it ever knit together?
HENRY	When it does, they cut it again. Keep it flowing.
KATE	How often?
HENRY	Once a month or so.
KATE	For how long?
HENRY	Since the accident, I guess . . . nine years ago? maybe ten?
KATE	Every month?
HENRY	Or so.

A moment.

KATE	Can I bathe it for you?
HENRY	You can't really want to do that.
KATE	I would do it for a sick dog. Why not for you. It'll hurt.
HENRY	I'm a man.
KATE	Good for you.

KATE opens a small wooden box and takes out an ointment. She places a towel under HENRY's leg. She fills a cup from the basin of water and irrigates the wound.

HENRY	*(picking up the box)* What's this?
KATE	It was my mother's. She kept her herbs in it.
HENRY	It's full of stones.
KATE	For healing.
HENRY	The shells, too?
KATE	Those are from trips to the seaside when I was a kid. And the freshwater pearls my mother gave me when I was little.

KATE smiles with the memory.

HENRY	What?

KATE   Oh, she had this big round pearl on a chain. She kept it in the top drawer of her dresser. I'd climb up on a stool and put it on, look in the mirror, when I knew she wasn't looking.

HENRY   Then how did she know to give you your own pearls if she wasn't looking?

KATE   Exactly.

HENRY   They have spies, mothers. Or eyes in the backs of their heads. The sides too. Just one big eye.

KATE laughs in spite of herself.

You were how old when she died?

KATE   Already married and living away.

KATE takes a pair of tweezers from the box, washes them, and picks bits out of the wound.

But we don't forget our parents, do we. What they did for us. Your girls'll remember too.

HENRY   That's none of your business.

KATE   You've made it my business. They have the right to be who they are, and you've taken that right away for political reasons. I disapprove of that. As their mother.

HENRY   Their mother? Has Mary heard you say that?

KATE   She will.

HENRY   Well, that disapproval is also noted. *(the leg)* It's a little hard to argue with you right now.

KATE   It must seriously hurt to walk on it.

HENRY   I'm a king.

KATE   A man *and* a king. Maybe there's a badge for that.

KATE applies the ointment.

From now on, when you're at home, you'll elevate it. I'll order some canes to be made.

HENRY   No.

KATE   Yes.

HENRY   Walking sticks on the public accounts? Too dangerous.

KATE   You have to take some pressure off this thing. Help it heal.

HENRY   I'm too fat.

KATE   You are what you are.

HENRY   It's too late to heal, Parr.

KATE   Never. Never too late to heal.

> *KATE is finished. Both of them are suddenly self-conscious, ashamed.*

HENRY   Are you going to cover it now?

KATE   Let it breathe.

HENRY   You'll get used to it.

KATE   Yes.

HENRY   Is this the time? you know, for us to . . . ?

KATE   No. But I appreciate your asking.

HENRY   I'm too fat.

KATE   You are what you are.

HENRY   You'll get used to it.

KATE   Yes.

SCENE SEVEN: A GAME OF TICKLE

At table. EDDIE *and* THOM *are on the ground, playing with two toy ships.*

EDDIE   *(making the waves)* Splsh. Splsh. Splsh.

THOM   Ahoy, matey! Swab up that poop!

EDDIE   Poop?!

THOM   Not that kind of poop. It's a deck. On the ship. Right here, see? Called the poop.

EDDIE   Why would they call it that?

THOM   Something to do with Latin. Splsh. Splsh. Splsh.

EDDIE   Oh! You're just saying it wrong. It's from the Latin, *puppis, meaning*: the stern of a vessel. Ahoy, matey! Swab up that *puppis*!

   KATE enters with books for her student.

   (to KATE*)* Hi.

KATE   Hello.

EDDIE   This is my new mother.

THOM   Hello.

EDDIE   This is my uncle Thommie.

KATE   Uncle Thommie.

THOM   Mother.

EDDIE   *(that's funny)* You don't call her mother.

THOM   I don't?

EDDIE   Her name is Katherine.

THOM   May I call her Kate.

EDDIE   Can he call you—oh! *May* he call you Kate?

KATE   May he. Yes. Uncle Thommie might call me Kate.

EDDIE   Not *your* Uncle Thommie. You call him Thomas. Or Thom.

KATE   Thom, then.

EDDIE   He brought me this! It's a ship. Not a boat.

> *EDDIE sits on the floor and plays with his toy.*

KATE   I thought it was writing time, Edward.

EDDIE   Can I play? Please? Just for a minute?

KATE   Just for a minute.

> *EDDIE plays. KATE and THOM take each other in.*

How's Holland?

EDDIE   He's working for my dad.

THOM   Lots of tulips.

KATE   All blonde?

EDDIE   *(that's funny)* Tulips are red.

> *EDDIE thinks.*

Or yellow.

THOM   And here?

KATE   I'm coping.

EDDIE   I'm writing letters.

THOM   Good.

> *A moment.*

KATE   You've come for meetings?

THOM   Strategic planning.

> *A moment.*

Is it a good game we're playing?

EDDIE   It's great!

KATE   Well, it's been pretty lonely, playing by myself, but now I know I still have someone to play with . . . it suddenly shows more promise.

EDDIE looks at KATE.

EDDIE   You can play with me. I like playing.

THOM suddenly tackles EDDIE. They play and laugh joyfully through the following section. It is all for KATE.

THOM   Ooooo, I miss you! I want to *wrestle* with you. I want to *cuddle* you. I want to lift up your top and *kiss your tummy*! I want to nibble right *here*! Ummummumm! Is that fun?

EDDIE   Do some more!

THOM   I want to . . .

EDDIE   Tickle me!

He does.

THOM   Yaaaaaah!

KATE   Blow on his back.

He does.

EDDIE laughs.

With your lips.

He does.

EDDIE laughs.

Make your fingers like spiders.

THOM   Like this?

EDDIE   / Yeah.

KATE   Skin on skin.

EDDIE   That's nice.

KATE   Now hold me.

EDDIE   Me.

          He does.

THOM   Like this?

KATE   Cradle my head.

          He does. A moment.

EDDIE   Now tickle me!

          And then it's awkward and over, and they sit in it for a moment.

THOM   I . . . better go.

EDDIE   Aawww, we're just having fun!

KATE   You and I have writing to practise. Uncle Thom will have to come back.

THOM   As soon as I can.

EDDIE   And bring another present?

THOM   Sure.

          THOM looks at KATE.

          (to EDDIE) Do I get a kiss?

          EDDIE kisses THOM on the lips.

EDDIE   I like my ships.

          THOM stands and looks at KATE.

THOM   Lips and ships.

          THOM waves at EDDIE. He goes. KATE stares after him for a moment, longingly. She moves slowly to the table. EDDIE sits at the table. He sees how distracted KATE is.

EDDIE	That was fun, wasn't it?
KATE	It sure was.
EDDIE	Don't be sad. He'll come back and we can play some more.
KATE	Yuh.
EDDIE	Wanna hear my letter?
KATE	I think so.

KATE sits beside EDDIE. EDDIE gives her a big cuddle. KATE isn't sure how to respond. EDDIE picks up his letter.

EDDIE	Okay, here goes:
	"Most honourable mother, I most / humbly"
KATE	Hang on.
EDDIE	What?
KATE	"Most honourable mother"? It makes me sound like a mean old bat or something. Couldn't it be less . . . formal?
EDDIE	It's an official letter.
KATE	But say, well, how you feel about me.
EDDIE	"Most honourable . . . *(writing)* and *entirely beloved* . . . mother . . . "
KATE	Oh! Really?
EDDIE	Is that not good?
KATE	No. That's good.
EDDIE	"I most humbly commend your grace with like thanks / both for . . . "
KATE	Hey, Eddie . . .
EDDIE	What.
KATE	Do you really think of me as your mother?

EDDIE	Sure.
KATE	Do you think Mary and Bess see me that way?
EDDIE	They should.
	"Both for that your grace did accept so gently my simple and rude letters, and / also"
KATE	So . . . do you think your father might accept them as his daughters again? you know, legally?
EDDIE	He never said they weren't his kids. He just calls them . . . *(whispers) It's a bad word.* But with you . . . it's like you're a mom for all of us. I think. And Father . . . well he's our dad. So that makes us a family: Mom, Dad, sisters, brother.
KATE	You are very smart.
EDDIE	I am.
KATE	We should just be a family.
EDDIE	Yes. If that's what the girls want.

SCENE EIGHT: ACT OF SUCCESSION/THE SUBMISSION OF LADY MARY: TO THE KING, HER FATHER

At table. KATE *and* MARY *are looking through an official document.*

MARY	Are you crazy? I won't do it. I don't need to be put in line with the bastards that badly.
KATE	It's a means to an end.
MARY	I don't want *the end.*
KATE	We've all had to take the oath / of obed—

MARY   You had to deny your mother?

KATE   I had to bow my will to his. If you / think

MARY   Hey! My mother's parents were Ferdinand and Isabella! I am descended from a *bona fide* line of both kings and queens. I don't need the permission of the great-grandson of the *bastard* of the *third son* of a king to assert my right.

KATE   Yes. You do.

MARY   Twenty-three years with one woman. Twenty. Three. Years. Of a loving marriage. Nine pregnancies they / had!

KATE   Nine? I did/n't

MARY   Stillbirths; miscarriages; Henry the Ninth—

> *MARY holds out her hand to indicate that he would have fit in it.*

this big—made it almost two months. Wouldn't you resort to binge eating? Fat and over forty: so he turns his back on her—on us—for a cheap young slut who'll keep his erection more / consistent.

KATE   Mary—

MARY   *That* killed my mother, you know.

What do I have left of her except my faith?

KATE   I get it. / But

MARY   Like you can.

KATE   the whole country's had to exchange their faith for this new one. Including me.

MARY   And you can reform. Just like that. Bully for you. You haven't lived with his whims your entire life.

KATE   Look, there's a series of articles. Go through them one at a / time.

MARY	I'm not going to / sign
KATE	His children are subjects / too.
MARY	Don't try to teach me, Kate! I'm a little old for you to act the mother. I'm not his child anymore, remember?
KATE	You're not his heir. That's what we're trying to change.
MARY	I— What's in this for you, anyway? Why are you on his side?
KATE	I'm on your side! I'm advocating for you! Will you help me do this. Please. Will you try.

MARY looks at the document on the table.

MARY	So . . . *if* I read the articles of the oath . . .
KATE	. . . as soon as you can swallow them in any way, put your pen to that paper. Don't look back.

* * *

In private. MARY reads the articles of the oath. Vulnerable.

MARY   "The confession of me, Lady Mary, in which I do now plainly and with all my heart declare my due conformity of obedience to the laws of the realm; I do most humbly beseech the King's Highness, my father, to forgive my obstinate and disobedient offences therein, and to take me to his most gracious mercy."

MARY hesitates, initials this paragraph, and reads on.

* * *

At table. KATE *with* HENRY.

KATE   Reinstate their succession.

HENRY   None of your business.

KATE   Eddie's too young.

HENRY   And I'm too old?

KATE   Your girls are healthy. Smart.

HENRY   They're bastards.

KATE   You don't mean that.

HENRY   Don't I.

KATE   You can't. What I remember of you . . . ?

HENRY   What you remember? Of me?

KATE   When Mary and I were girls. You were impossibly tall. Handsome. Funny.

HENRY   I was never funny.

KATE   Dancing a galliard? you were pretty funny.

HENRY   A galliard?

KATE   At a masque in the great hall. I hid in my mother's skirts. The queen made you laugh, then you grabbed Mary, stood her on your feet, and danced—this giant clown.

HENRY   I was drunk.

KATE   You probably were. You gave us each a piece of unicorn horn. I still have mine.

HENRY   The unicorn horn; that was you?

KATE   That was me.

HENRY   How about that.

A moment.

KATE   The way you looked at her. Even as a child, I thought . . . that must be love.

HENRY   She was my little doll.

KATE   No, no. At Katherine. At Aragon.

HENRY   Pick the wound, why don't you.

* * *

In private. MARY.

MARY   "I confess and acknowledge the King's Majesty to be my sovereign lord and king of this realm of England; and do submit myself to His Highness and to each and every law and statute of this realm, as it becomes a true and faithful subject to do."

MARY initials this paragraph.

* * *

In private. KATE *with* BESS. *A document sits on the table in front of* BESS.

BESS   But he hates me.

KATE   He doesn't.

BESS   If he'd just stayed with Mary's mom, none of this would have happened.

KATE   None of what would have happened?

BESS	He wouldn't have sent me away.
KATE	If you want to be a princess again, Bess, you have to sign this paper.
BESS	What does it say?
KATE	That you'll do what he asks of you.
BESS	Did you agree to do that?
KATE	It'll be a lot easier to get your succession reinstated if you pretend you like him.
BESS	But I thought I was trying to get back my status, not give it away.
KATE	It's give and take.
BESS	Oh? What's he giving up for me?
KATE	Some of the things he's said in the past, I hope.
BESS	Like, that my mother had sex with her brother?
KATE	I doubt it.
BESS	Or that I look like her and that's why he hates me?
KATE	That's not true.
BESS	He said it. Twice.
KATE	Your father loves all his children.
BESS	He does not. He hates Mary too.
KATE	He loves Mary too. But, like you, she reminds him of all the brutal and ruthless things he's done.

* * *

In private. MARY.

MARY   "I do recognize, accept, and acknowledge the King's Highness to be supreme head on earth, under Christ, of the Church of England; and do utterly refuse *the bishop of Rome's* pretended authority, power, and jurisdiction within this realm."

Can't even call him the bloody pope! Idiot.

MARY reluctantly initials this paragraph.

* * *

At table. KATE *with* HENRY.

KATE   The country needed stability: to leave England with a future king? with a helmsman? Having a son was imperative.

HENRY   Imperative is right. *Jane* gave me Eddie. *Jane* gave the country security.

KATE   Yes, but if Eddie died tomor/row

HENRY   Don't / you

KATE   *If,* I said: there would be civil war—anarchy—until one of your beloved council ended up as heir. If you reinstate the girls, the course is clear, and your bloodline stays on the throne.

HENRY   For starters, a *king*dom is just that.

I can't go back on my word.

KATE   You change your mind at the drop of a hat.

HENRY   Gently now.

KATE regroups.

KATE   The girls might forgive you if they understood your motives.

HENRY   I don't need their forgiveness.

KATE   We all need forgiveness. Tell them you chose divorce and murder for the good of the / country

HENRY   annulment and / execution

KATE   for the higher good. They can understand that choice.

HENRY   It was hardly altruistic. The fact that it suited my carnal desires so completely has nothing to do with it. The fact that I've killed young girls because they fuck around on me has no correlation to my incompetence as a man. All for England! I'm fat, cranky, and my leg is rotting; who wouldn't fuck around on me, eh, Parr?!

KATE   No, no, no: you don't want me to die like that Howard girl. You don't want to kill another innocent woman. You love women, Hal, don't you.

HENRY   Do I.

KATE   You love strong women.

HENRY   Like you?

KATE   Like Mary. Like Bess.

* * *

In private. MARY. *Vulnerable.*

MARY "I do freely, frankly, and for the discharge of my duty towards God, the King's Highness, and his laws, recognize and acknowledge that the marriage formerly had between His Majesty and my mother . . . was by God's law . . . and man's law . . . incestuous and unlawful."

MARY *doesn't move.*

* * *

In private. KATE *with* BESS.

BESS Get away from me! I won't do it! I don't see why I should be nice to him when he's so mean to me!

KATE To get what your mother wanted for you.

BESS You don't know what my mother wanted.

KATE You're right. I know . . . my mother wanted me to have all the opportunities that were available, so guess what she did.

BESS I don't care.

A moment, while curiosity gets the best of her.

What did she do?

KATE She taught me Plutarch; how to lance a boil; the names of herbs in Latin. Does that sound good?

BESS No.

KATE	Not at all. I had no idea when she did those things that they'd be good for me. I had to trust her. I had to believe that she did them because she loved me.
BESS	But you don't even know me.
KATE	I think I do. A bit.
	You don't really have to forgive him. Just start by thinking that what he did then, he did as your king, and if he does this, it's because he's your dad. Do you remember him just being your dad?

BESS thinks about all this.

BESS	Do you think girls are smart enough to run a country?
KATE	Girls are smart. They just aren't legal.

A moment.

BESS	I remember sitting on his lap.
KATE	Do you.
BESS	I'd dropped my lollipop in the dirt, and I was crying. I remember that. He picked me up.

* * *

At table. KATE with HENRY.

HENRY	She loved my ermine waistcoat. She would suck her thumb and rub the nap. Her skin was the softest skin I've ever touched. She smelled like honey.
	Why is that?
KATE	Hal . . .

HENRY   If you have to choose between your daughters and your country . . . you choose your country. Ask any leader.

* * *

In private. MARY *signs the final article. Looks at the page.*
Spits on it. Hands it to KATE.

MARY   So what he did is right.

* * *

BESS *signs the document. Hands it to* KATE.

BESS   So what he did is right.

* * *

At table. KATE *with* HENRY. KATE *hands* HENRY *the signed*
documents.

KATE   So what you did is right.

HENRY   Of course it's not right. They know that. You know that. I'm
not an idiot.

KATE   Then at least make it right for them. They're your blood, Hal.
Give them that. Give yourself that.

* * *

In public. HENRY reads his proclamation.

HENRY His Highness, most prudently and wisely considering and calling to his remembrance how this realm standeth in the case of succession, thinketh it convenient that in case it shall happen the king and the said excellent Prince Edward, to decease without heir of either of their bodies lawfully begotten, the imperial crown and all other the premises shall first to the Lady Mary, the king's daughter, and to the heirs of the body of the same Lady Mary lawfully begotten; and for default of such issue the said imperial crown and other the premises shall be to the Lady Elizabeth, the king's second daughter, and to the heirs of the body of the said Lady Elizabeth lawfully begotten; anything to the contrary of this act notwithstanding.

* * *

At table. KATE contemplates her success.

SCENE NINE: THREE-WAY

At table. HENRY and THOM. HENRY signs off on an official document.

HENRY You see it all comes down to the stud. Race horses, you know: they'll breed hundreds of mares to one stallion, but if the babies can run . . . okay, the mother's there in the small print, but the *bloodline* follows the sire. Am I right?

THOM	I don't know. I've never been to the track.
HENRY	Patriarchy is part of nature. Why ignore that.
	So I changed the law. To recognize my bloodline. It makes a lot of sense to me.
THOM	That's what matters.
HENRY	And where did you say the fleet is readied?
THOM	Just coastwise of Rotterdam, in the Beer Canal.
HENRY	The Beer Canal?! Hah! Good job!

KATE walks in with some books. She stops upon seeing THOM.

	(to THOM) Guns and ammunition loaded?
THOM	All the ships can carry.
HENRY	Kate! You remember Thomas. He's got our boats in the Beer Canal!
KATE	Does he. Very funny.
THOM	Though should we enter battle, Your Majesty, reinforcements will certainly be necessary.
HENRY	We're just finishing up.
KATE	I'll leave you to it.
HENRY	No, no, we're on our way. I was just telling Thom how necessary it is that I've changed my mind.
KATE	About what?
HENRY	About what?!— I've reversed an Act of Parliament. Because of you!
KATE	Yes, / I
HENRY	You're influencing the king.
KATE	*(to THOM)* It's true. I am.

HENRY	Get a wife, Thom. They're remarkable.
THOM	I will. Soon, I hope.
HENRY	Showing me a new path, she is. A more fruitful path.
KATE	Possibilities, that's all.
HENRY	And it's good. Keeps me on my toes. It's not exactly annexing land, or creaming the French, or anything exciting, but . . .
KATE	It's helping the girls.
HENRY	That's right. You've helped the girls. Aren't you pleased?
KATE	Of course I am.
HENRY	And Eddie. *(to THOM)* Have you seen him lately? Suddenly smarter than me!

HENRY kisses KATE. He takes both KATE and THOM by the hand.

	You two. Very useful to me. That doesn't go unnoticed. Anything else here, Thom?
THOM	Nothing, sir.
HENRY	Right then: let's get to Council: we've got a war to plan, and a country to run.

HENRY goes. THOM and KATE share a charged moment. THOM follows HENRY.

SCENE TEN: FAMILY DINNER

At table. KATE, HENRY, MARY, BESS, and EDDIE. EDDIE is the only one still eating. HENRY has his leg up and canes that look like souped-up curtain rods by his side.

BESS	Are you happy, Majesty?
HENRY	What?

KATE	Tell your father what we were studying this morning.
BESS	The ethics of Aristotle.
KATE	Which are based on . . . ?
BESS	The cardinal virtues of Plato:
HENRY	Smarty-pants.
BESS	Courage, temperance, justice, and . . . / prudence.
EDDIE	*(with a mouthful)* Prudence.
HENRY	Dear prudence.
KATE	And the practice of these virtues is to achieve . . . ?
BESS	The highest human good.
KATE	Referred to by Aristotle as . . . ?
BESS	Happiness.
HENRY	*(answering BESS's first question)* No.
BESS	Yes. That's what Mother taught us today.
HENRY	Mother?
KATE	*(regarding the lesson)* You've confused the child, Majesty.
MARY	*(correcting BESS)* Her Grace.
BESS	Her Grace.
HENRY	*(picking up BESS's idea)* No, no: Mother. Are we a family here or a court? Am I your husband or your king?
KATE	I . . . Both.
HENRY	Yeah. Can we call each other by name please. Can I have the opportunity, on occasion, to be a . . . dad.
KATE	Of course.
HENRY	No, I am not happy. Bess.
BESS	Oh.

MARY	I can't imagine why you wouldn't be happy. Dad. You're the king of all you survey.
HENRY	Don't get cocky, kiddo. You're being insufferable here at the invitation of Mother, not me.
KATE	Hal.
MARY	You're right. I am here for Her Grace. Kate. Mother. Certainly not for you.
HENRY	I am not happy—and neither is Mary—because true happiness requires an excellent character. And an excellent character / is a
BESS	is achieved by virtue of what we undertake voluntarily, and not what we accomplish under duress.
HENRY	Yup.

HENRY *I am sitting at luncheon with the three of you women, under duress.* My son and I could be overseeing plans for the impending invasion of France: a perfectly manly pastime. I would *undertake* that pastime *voluntarily* but I cannot because my fucking leg is killing me and I'm left to hobble around with the help of souped-up curtain rods, *under duress.*

Ergo, I do not possess an excellent character. *Ergo,* I am not happy.

MARY	Perhaps your humour is too hot.
HENRY	Aaaaah, heat—hang on a sec, now—heat—the choleric humour—is a quality possessed more by men than by women, and makes a person more intelligent.

HENRY *(to BESS)* Did you read that part?

MARY	More subject to a tyrannical nature.
HENRY	*(to KATE)* A woman is cold—melancholic—and therefore more deceptive.

BESS   How is Mother deceptive?

HENRY   A woman who gives a child the means to provoke her father under the guise of education. That is deceptive.

KATE   *(coming back at HENRY)* A deceptive person is one who skirts the truth.

BESS   But she's not trying to provoke you; she's trying to make you happy. Mother says if you were more balanced, if you saw things as less black and white and / more

HENRY   Hang on; you talk about me in your studies, do you?

BESS   You are the king. We use you as an example of wisdom and leadership.

HENRY   *(playing along)* Uhuh. And in an analysis of my wisdom and leadership you feel that my policies are too . . . ?

BESS   Inflexible.

KATE   We / don't

HENRY   Ah. And your mother's advice to me would be . . . ?

BESS   To see both sides of the coin, be/cause

HENRY   More grey.

BESS   Yes.

KATE   In the ab/stract

HENRY   More lenience. More . . . tolerance.

BESS   Yes.

KATE   Theoretically.

HENRY   If I travelled the golden mean, for instance . . .

BESS   Yes!

        (to KATE) He *does* know.

HENRY   Right. You want to learn a lesson. Get your notebook . . .

HENRY grabs BESS by the arm. EDDIE stops eating.

BESS   Ow.

HENRY   GET YOUR NOTEBOOK!

(to BESS, but looking at KATE) Write this down: Aristotle wasn't an Englishman. Nor did he have to deal with the fucking Catholics.

BESS looks to KATE. EDDIE covers his ears and closes his eyes.

WRITE IT DOWN!

BESS   I told you!

MARY goes.

HENRY   *(calling after her)* You're supposed to excuse yourself from the presence of your goddamn king!

MARY returns.

MARY   Will you pardon me, Your Majesty, my stomach has taken / a turn.

HENRY   Yeah. Piss off.

MARY   *(turning back sharply)* That "submission" I signed? It's just a contract: like your marriage: no truth in it. When you're dead you can't touch my faith, and you can't touch what I know about my mother. You *will* die—hopefully soon—and when you do, I'll rip those lies out of my body.

(to KATE) You know the family portrait he commissioned last month? He had *Jane* painted in as our mother. Just in case you thought you were getting somewhere.

KATE is hurt by this choice of HENRY's. MARY goes.

HENRY   *(after her)* Frigid Catholic Bitch!

KATE   Teach me the lesson, will you? The girls are just doing what I tell them.

HENRY	*(of BESS)* Parroting her like this . . . Don't try to dangle your ethics in front of me. I'm not a fish to be baited.
KATE	Go to your room, / Bess.
HENRY	*(to BESS)* Don't you dare!
	See how your "mother" is using you to get what she wants?
	(to KATE) I am not to be steered, woman. You may have operated this way in the past, but you'll have to be a lot more canny with me.
	(to BESS) That's the last lesson you'll be learning here. Go. Pack a bag. You're back to Hatfield tomorrow.
KATE	/ No
BESS	No
KATE	Henry, don't. She's a child.
HENRY	*(to KATE)* DON'T USE THE CHILDREN!
KATE	I'm not using them!
BESS	*(to KATE)* Yes you are! This is your fault! You want me to think like you. You want me to want what you want and do what you do. But I can't; I can't; I'm not smart enough.
KATE	/ You are
BESS	I Can't Be You!
	BESS runs from the room.
HENRY	Talk to *me*! what do you *want*?
KATE	I didn't mean to use—I, I was trying to show them options, that's / all.
HENRY	Oh, for God's sake, woman! Have you ever had absolute power?! Do you really think the options aren't glaringly obvious?!

Get your shit together, Kate. You've lost your little wedding present now. Let's hope you fare better with Eddie.

HENRY leaves. EDDIE slowly takes his hands off his ears and opens his eyes.

SCENE ELEVEN: SAILOR BOY

In private. KATE enters. THOM is there: in his cups, sloppy, and an emotional wreck.

KATE What are you doing?!

THOM Drink/ing.

KATE How did you get in here—are you nuts?! Did anyone see / you?

THOM I'm nuts. I love / you.

KATE You're drunk.

THOM I'm a sea captain.

KATE Yo ho ho.

THOM I had to see you.

KATE If you're caught?

THOM You don't want to see me?

KATE I want to run away with you—right now!

THOM I'm not strong like you.

KATE What?

THOM He kisses you!

KATE What did you expect?

THOM I can't watch that. How come it doesn't bug you?

KATE	Doesn't—? Look. I—can't deal with— Can I just feel sorry for myself for one minute without having to deal with another deprived child?
	I hate this / whole
THOM	/ I love you
KATE	I gain one ounce of his respect, and then . . . I take the whole ship down with me.
THOM	At least you're influencing the king; what am I doing? following orders again, and it's, it's like I see you once every three months and you don't even want me here.

THOM reaches for KATE and tries to kiss her.

	I love / you.
KATE	Must you resort to groping?
THOM	I wasn't / groping
KATE	Sorry. I'm . . .

KATE takes THOM's hand.

	It's a relief to me when we just . . . breathe the same air, sit in the same room. It's . . .
THOM	Not intimate.
KATE	It's the most intimate.
THOM	Not the most, trust me. And he's . . . touching the places that . . . I'm thinking about . . .
KATE	He's not.
THOM	Why do you bother with me?
KATE	I don't know, okay? Not right at this moment. But if you'll just sit with me for a while, maybe I can figure that out.
	You're completely different from him. You're . . . well, something . . . simple.

THOM   I'm not sim/ple!

KATE   Uncomplicated I mean. That's good. That's a lot.

THOM   He's too big. I can't compete. I'm not . . . man enough.

KATE   What a ridiculous thing to say. There's nothing to compete with.

> *HENRY is heard singing in the distance.* KATE *and* THOM'S *dialogue overlaps.*

HENRY   "Whoso that will all feats obtain
        In love he must be without disdain.
        For love reinforces what's noble kind,
        And disdain discourages the gentle mind."

KATE   Oh God. Get out. Hurry.

> THOM *is slow to move.*

        Thom. Come on! You have to get out of here!

> *He resists.*

THOM   I don't want this anymore.

KATE   Don't say that. It's the booze.

THOM   No. I don't care. It's not like I'm in love with you.

> THOM *goes . . .*

SCENE TWELVE: RENAISSANCE MAN

> *. . . and* HENRY *enters. He stands for a moment.* KATE *is not sure if she's been caught.*

HENRY   I wrote that song.

KATE   I like it.

HENRY	Not for you, but. When I was younger.
KATE	Uhuh. It's nice. To hear you sing.

A moment.

HENRY	You alone?
KATE	I'm . . . in my room.
HENRY	Yes, I . . . thought maybe the girls . . .
KATE	No, I looked in on them. And Eddie.
HENRY	Good.
KATE	And now I'm here. Alone.

HENRY goes out.

Where are / you . . . ?

HENRY	*(from off)* Hang on.

HENRY is humming all the while and then comes back with a bottle of wine and two glasses. He pours, hands a glass to KATE, and sings.

"Why when our love is not returned
Do we crave death? We have a lesson to learn:
All love gives courage, and makes one bold;
Disdain abates and makes him cold . . .
Great pity it is that we love compel
With disdain, both false and subtle."

KATE	Quite the troubadour.
HENRY	Yeah, hnh, I was, when I was a kid. *(à la rock star)* I, uh . . . wrote a few tunes, you know.
KATE	I'd like to meet that kid.
HENRY	He moved on; made way for the king.
KATE	So . . . who did you write it for?

HENRY	Katherine. Aragon.
KATE	You—?
HENRY	She needed some encouraging.
	You see, when my brother died . . . well, she had to be married to the king or peace with Spain would go out the window. And she wasn't nuts about marrying his greaseball kid brother who played the local coffee houses on a Sunday night.
KATE	So you wrote her a song about love and death?
HENRY	I was fifteen. It's all about love and death when you're fifteen, right?
KATE	*(she's never known those feelings)* Right.
	They drink.
HENRY	But that's not—I sang the song for you because of this part—
	"Great pity it is that we love compel With disdain, both false and subtle."
	That's me. At dinner. Compelling you. With disdain, when . . . And— Look, I . . . I owe you an apology.
KATE	I . . . uh . . . beg your pardon?
HENRY	I'm apologizing.
KATE	For . . . ? before. Oh. Well. I'm not exactly . . . blame/less
HENRY	My leg was driving me nuts, and I wanted to be on manoeuvres with Eddie, and . . . all you women around, I just . . .
	I behaved badly.
	I'm sorry.
	Honest.
KATE	I accept your apology.
HENRY	Right, but will you forgive me. I need your forgiveness.

A moment.

KATE   There are things about you I don't understand.

HENRY   With good reason.

KATE   You can be so . . .

HENRY   Sexy?

KATE   I was going to say impossible.

HENRY   Fair.

KATE   And then you can come in here singing some little ditty you penned and throw me a total curveball.

A moment.

I feel like I don't get to have an opinion.

HENRY   You do. You absolutely do. You just have to convince me that I should have it too.

KATE   And Bess?

HENRY   Collateral.

KATE   That's a hard lesson.

HENRY   It is.

A moment.

Will you forgive me.

KATE   Will you forgive me?

HENRY   Yes.

KATE   Yes.

HENRY   Yay.

They smile. They drink.

KATE   So you never expected to be king.

HENRY   I never wanted to be king.

KATE	Hmm. It must make you . . . lonely. Sometimes.
HENRY	Lonely?
KATE	I . . .

What you've given up. Having no . . . friends.

HENRY	Just wives. So have a bunch of them.
KATE	I'll remember that.
HENRY	Well come on: your great string of husbands?
KATE	Three!
HENRY	There. See? Something in common.
KATE	You've had six!
HENRY	Sure, but . . . third-time lucky.
KATE	Oh.
HENRY	And you are lucky! I come from a civilized family / not
KATE	You / what?!
HENRY	not one of your bloody northerners.
KATE	Hey! There's nothing wrong with northerners! And what are you? Part Welsh?!
HENRY	Dim ond y rhan ddoniol! [Only the funny part.]
KATE	What?
HENRY	It'll lose in the translation.

They laugh.

You laugh now, but if you tell anyone I said these things, I'll have to kill you.

A moment.

More wine?

A moment.

You think I'm joking.

A moment.

KATE   That kid, that musician . . .

HENRY   What about him.

KATE   Tell him I like his song.

HENRY   Wouldn't know him if I fell over him.

        HENRY touches KATE as gently as he can. KATE takes his hand.

KATE   *(just facts)* I might panic. Just so you know. I might not be able to. Sometimes all I can see is them. Even with my eyes shut. I may have to stop, and then you . . . you have to stop, too.

HENRY   I will.

        A silence. KATE kisses HENRY's hand.

KATE   Can I bathe you? Let me bathe your leg.

        KATE leads HENRY to the bed.

SCENE THIRTEEN: OMEN

        At bed. KATE and HENRY are asleep. EDDIE runs into the room. HENRY watches this scene unfold, barely breathing.

EDDIE   Mommy?!

KATE   Eddie—

EDDIE   There was blood—

KATE   On you?

EDDIE   He was trying to hurt you / and

KATE   All right—

EDDIE   and I couldn't get to you

KATE	I'm okay—
EDDIE	No, your neck, and I was too little
KATE	Okay now—
EDDIE	and he could just hold me back with one hand
KATE	Here—
EDDIE	and I couldn't get to you 'cause I wasn't strong enough
KATE	All right now—
EDDIE	I couldn't help you!
KATE	I'm not hurt—
EDDIE	But there was blood on you! there was blood on you!
KATE	See? I'm fine.

EDDIE settles.

EDDIE	There was blood on you.
KATE	It was a dream.
EDDIE	It was a bad dream.
KATE	A very bad dream.
EDDIE	Yeah.
KATE	Yeah. Okay now?
EDDIE	Okay. Yeah.
KATE	Wanna sleep in the big bed?
EDDIE	Yeah.
KATE	Come on then.

EDDIE crawls in beside KATE.

I have something that will help with those scary dreams.

EDDIE	You do?

KATE   A little present for you.

EDDIE   Okay.

> *KATE brings out a miniature portrait.*

It's you. It's both of you. And look: it fits in my pocket.

> *EDDIE puts the portrait in his pocket.*

KATE   No more bad dreams, right?

EDDIE   Right.

KATE   You are strong and smart and capable.

EDDIE   I'm scared at night. And look:

> *EDDIE shows his muscles.*

KATE   When people tell you you're weak, it's because they're afraid of you. Maybe not of what your body can do, but what . . . what the stuff inside you can do. You and me, we're not strong like your dad, but inside—deep in here *(EDDIE's heart)*; in here *(KATE's heart)*—we know that no one can push us around. Can you believe that?

EDDIE   Yeah.

KATE   Good. Sleep now.

> *KATE tucks EDDIE into bed. KATE and HENRY watch him sleep.*

SCENE FOURTEEN: REGENT

> *In private. KATE and HENRY are dressing in formal attire. In mid-debate.*

KATE   But who's gonna lead the forces?

HENRY   Me.

KATE   See—that's ridiculous—from here?

HENRY   How can I lead an invasion from here, woman.

KATE   You can't *go*.

HENRY   You've made me well enough.

KATE   Your leg is slightly better.

HENRY   I've lost weight, too. All the humping.

KATE   Your horse won't be that grateful.

           There are people better suited to go to France. What if you die there?

HENRY   I might win security for my kingdom. Is that at all a possibility in your mind?

KATE   And the Council? What do they think of this plan?

HENRY   They think I'm a lousy soldier. Always have.

KATE   Well then . . . ?

HENRY   This is important to me.

KATE   I'm listening.

HENRY   It's my last chance, Parr. To prove my strength. Before the young bucks take me down.

           A moment.

KATE   Okay then. You go. You gotta go.

HENRY   You think so?

KATE   I do.

HENRY   Will I die there?

KATE   Not from the leg.

HENRY   Good then. And by the grace of God, I'll see you by autumn.

KATE   And the children?

HENRY	Them too.
KATE	Will I have their guardianship?
HENRY	Bess is at Hatfield—
KATE	And how much longer are you imposing that sentence?
HENRY	Mary takes care of herself.
KATE	So will I care for Eddie? While you're gone?
HENRY	Edward will have a regent. According to the law.
KATE	Yes.
HENRY	Your beau's older brother, I expect.
KATE	Ted Seymour?
HENRY	The Council will decide.
KATE	*(planting a thought)* Not if you decide for them.
	A moment.
HENRY	What, *you*? A regent?
KATE	I'd be honoured to protect your son.
HENRY	It's not a job for a woman.
KATE	What a stupid thing to say.
HENRY	The Council's used to things a certain way. We have a shorthand.
KATE	You mean your cronies might have to be polite.
HENRY	It's a man thing: defending the pack. It requires aggression.
KATE	I can be aggressive.
HENRY	You're not very attractive when you are. Even in that dress.
	HENRY zips up KATE's dress.
	Okay. Maybe in that dress.

The Council won't follow a woman.

KATE   You left Aragon as regent.

HENRY   That was thirty years ago. I was in slightly better shape.

KATE   And she was only protecting a girl.

HENRY   Oh, don't let's go down that road again.

>   *KATE is struggling with her bracelet.*

KATE   You're the one who started it: not a job for a woman.

HENRY   There are jobs that men can't do too.

>   *HENRY beckons for KATE's wrist.*

Let me.

>   *She obliges.*

KATE   Name one. And don't say cooking, or cleaning, or nursing, or teaching, or raising kids, or delivering babies or shovelling snow or get/ting the groceries

HENRY   Snow? I shovel snow!

KATE   *You* shovel snow?

HENRY   I have a *man* that shovels snow. I don't see *you* out there in your mittens and toque.

KATE   The point is: you kill people *and* you do handcrafts.

HENRY   You want to kill people?

KATE   No! I want to have the *authority* to show you that you don't have to!

HENRY   And that's exactly why you can't have it! You can't just flip the entire system on its head.

KATE   Why not?

HENRY   Because, well . . . because we understand how it works this way! If you have no realistic plan to change the rules then,

then you have to follow the rules that are in place. Just like I do.

KATE   I do have a realistic plan: make me regent for Eddie. The whole reason you married me is to educate him, and to see him on the throne. That's what you've *trusted* me with from the start.

HENRY   Arranging for teachers around the palace, and protecting a future king from the threats of his enemies require different qualifications.

KATE   So you trust Ted Seymour to protect and train your son.

HENRY   No.

KATE   You trust your Council to choose an adequate regent, then.

HENRY   I trust no one.

KATE   Then I guess you're taking him with you.

HENRY   Don't be ridiculous.

KATE   What choice do you have?

HENRY   Who do *you* trust?

KATE   I trust you, Hal.

HENRY   Me? Why on earth would you trust me?

KATE   Because you chose me as your wife.

        KATE scores the point.

HENRY   Ooooh, you're sharp.

KATE   Because for thirty-six years you've led this country—not without a few bumps in the road—but basically forward.

HENRY   There's a sound endorsement.

KATE   You may not be wise, but you're sure smart.

HENRY   Oh, I like you, Parr.

KATE Don't hurt yourself.

HENRY Whoever is regent of Eddie while I'm gone will likely be regent of the kingdom.

KATE That makes sense, since Eddie is the future of the kingdom.

HENRY They would have to submit one hundred percent to the advice of the Privy Council. The appointed regent couldn't possibly see this as some triumph of gender rights, or personal freedoms, or any other political hokum.

KATE Yes. I agree with that. The highly distasteful men on your Council have years of experience with the parliament, the country, and all the current affairs. It would be short-sighted of anyone to see the regency as a means of asserting one's individual authority. A regent is merely a proxy for the wishes of the king.

To be directed by someone who is familiar with those wishes.

Who supports those wishes.

Who trusts those wishes.

HENRY The smart choice would be Ted Seymour.

KATE I can see that. Yes. That would certainly be the smart choice.

SCENE FIFTEEN: HENRY VIII'S COMMISSION FOR PAYMENT OF MONIES BY QUEEN KATHERINE AS REGENT

In public. HENRY *holds* KATE's *hand.* MARY *and* EDDIE *look on.*

HENRY To all, et cetera.

Henry VIII, et cetera.

Know ye, that taking our voyage at this present over the seas to invade the realm of France, we have in our absence ordained our most dearest and most entirely beloved wife, Queen Katherine, to be Regent General of this our realm; from which position she may oversee our treasury, and defray sundry sums of money that must instantly be made for our affairs. My Lord of Hertford, Edward Seymour, shall be made her lieutenant-in-case, to supervise the security of this our kingdom, taking his commission for that purpose *by the authority* of the Queen Regent, our said most dearest wife.

God save and protect Katherine the Queen.

MARY &
EDDIE God save and protect Katherine the Queen.

ACT TWO
SCENE SIXTEEN: TRAINING DAY

At table. KATE *and* MARY *are sitting amid stacks of books and papers in the Situation Room. There is a flurry of administrative activity.* BESS *brings in a hefty report.*

MARY   What is that?

BESS   A comparison of the cargo differentials of a hoy and crayer.

MARY   Who would have dreamed.

KATE   Let's see, Bess.

MARY   *(of* BESS*)* I keep forgetting you're back.

BESS   Did you miss me?

MARY   Let's say yes.

KATE   *I* missed you.

BESS   Good.

       (to MARY*)* This is fun. It makes me happy.

MARY   I haven't been happy since you were born.

BESS   Sorry.

KATE	Mary.
MARY	Don't apologize: your birth can't possibly be construed as being your fault.
BESS	Okay.

MARY hugs and kisses BESS.

MARY	I don't blame you; I just don't like you.
BESS	I wish you wouldn't say things like that when you're hugging me.
KATE	*(looking at the report)* They're not sturdy enough to ship the cannons.
MARY	The Council?
KATE	The navy. Now what. It's a bit pointless to ship the lead and the shovels and not send the cannons.
BESS	Sloops . . .
MARY	Sloops?
BESS	What about trading ships?
MARY	Why bother with all this in the first place?
KATE	Enlist the merchants?
BESS	It's to protect their country. They won't have any trade if they have no country.

KATE closes her eyes, holds her head in her hands.

KATE	I can't see straight anymore.

BESS locates two large volumes from a pile of books. She places one in front of MARY and takes one for herself.

MARY	"Cargo Analysis for Merchant Mariners." Yippee.
KATE	Don't moan.
MARY	I said / yippee.

BESS	To work, Mary! A busy hive with three queens!
MARY	Three what?
BESS	Well, Mother is already Queen, and you and I . . . I mean, either one of us *could* be.
MARY	Could be—?
BESS	There's the possibility.
MARY	Of Father dying?
BESS	No.
	But. Maybe. Eddie.
MARY	Eddie?
KATE	*(still in the books)* It's easier to read Hebrew than all these bloody acronyms.
BESS	*(as if quoting a report)* Nearly seventy percent of the male offspring in our extended family have died before their eighteenth birthday.
	KATE stops what she is doing.
KATE	Really?
MARY	Wow. A little hungry, Bess?
BESS	The earth nurtures nothing so fragile as *man.* That's what Homer said. We should be ready.
MARY	For what?
KATE	You have the right to succeed.
MARY	Awh crap, don't tell me you're buying this garbage.
KATE	You have opportunity and position.
MARY	You've certainly stepped into your opportunity. And created yourself quite the tidy little position. You didn't show this kind of ambition when we were girls.

KATE	My reach is limited.
MARY	So this is your little School for Queens?
BESS	Hey, that's exactly what it / is!
MARY	So that, what, we can bargain away our own cherry instead of them doing it for us?
KATE	*(to BESS)* If you're ever queen you'll make / far more
MARY	*Queen.* By whose ordinance? Under what conditions? Once her father's dead? and her brother's dead? Once I'm dead? What are / you—?
KATE	Show a little gratitude. I've changed the rules for you!
MARY	So should we lock the little prince in the tower?
BESS	That's / not
MARY	Get the Council on side? Have them sign the papers?
BESS	Mary.
MARY	Come on, Bess. Eddie gets the prize cuz he's a boy. Don't you hate him for that?
BESS	No.
MARY	Isn't that what this *exercise* is about, Kate? How we hate the men? How they *use* us? how we suffer such indignities at their hands? We should hate them: using us to strike allegiances, garner contracts; we're like toys to them, playthings—let alone that they raped you / for
KATE	Mary—!
MARY	jurisdiction over a field in Northumberland. That must leave a nasty taste.
BESS	Is that true?

MARY   And as for me: now that I'm no longer a national asset no man wants to marry me for my shining personality. How pleasing a life we live. I shall dance and sing: huzzah!

BESS   Am I a national asset?

MARY   You're young: you may yet be bought and paid for as border security.

KATE   What you will have, Bess, / is

MARY   What she will *have*? Hogwash. You're misleading her, / Kate.

KATE   Just— Listen! You're so close to the crown! Both of you! You are so close to showing what—what you can do. I— They owe you that much for what's been done to you in the name of this country.

MARY   Queen School Lesson One: Take England from the Men.

        THOM enters.

THOM   Your Majesty. Your Highnesses.

MARY   *(startled)* Good grief, were you skulking in the corner?

BESS   Thom! Hi! How's Holland? Are there good parties? Wow. I hear their music is great.

THOM   You, Bess, would love it.

        I'm—uh—on my way to Wulfhall actually; quick turnaround. His Majesty has called for my assistance in France.

KATE   Has he? Called for you?

        BESS shows KATE an entry in her book.

BESS   Is this what / we're . . . ?

THOM   And there's something that came up at Council this / morning that

KATE   One sec . . .

        She looks at the entry.

	(to BESS) We can't hoist the cannons. They need to be rolled.
THOM	Can I help? You . . . look like you could use my help.
KATE	We're fine. We'll manage.
THOM	I know a thing or two about ships is all.
BESS	You can help / me!
KATE	We're learning. We're good. Thank you.
THOM	I don't mean / to be
MARY	She's a bit defensive just now. I've put a stick in her craw.
KATE	You said. Something that came up . . . ?
THOM	Pertaining to Council business.
BESS	The regent is in! Step this way!
THOM	Well, thank you so much. And who are you, young lady?
BESS	I'm a princess.
THOM	Well, I beg your pardon.
BESS	Assistant to the regent.
THOM	Quite the title: *(bows)* Your Highness Assistant Regent.
BESS	*(nods)* Sir Thomas.
THOM	*(to KATE)* I . . . uh, may I speak openly?
KATE	On matters of business.
THOM	I just wonder if you're taking the wrong course with this . . . invasion of the West Country.
BESS	Invasion?!
KATE	*Rumoured* invasion. What do you mean, the wrong course?
THOM	Maybe you should tell the king the whole story. If he finds out, he may be . . . disappointed with the way you've handled it. I can take him a message when I go to France.

BESS	I bet they have great parties in France.
MARY	*(to BESS)* Zip it.
BESS	Okayyyy.
KATE	The king doesn't need to know details. It would distract him.
THOM	You see, that's— The Council's concerned.
KATE	Why?
THOM	That you're setting a dangerous precedent.
KATE	This is my thing. I'm doing this.
MARY	*(to BESS)* Lesson Two: How to Be an Autocrat.
THOM	It's, it's an indictable offence to mislead the king.
KATE	I'm not misleading the king.
THOM	Your actions aren't entirely honest.
KATE	My actions are honest: they're just not explicit.
THOM	You're withholding information that concerns national security.
KATE	Yes, but— No. I don't think it does concern national security; that's my point. I don't think full disclosure is the best policy, in this case. Do you?
THOM	You don't want to catch him off guard.
KATE	No, I'm trying to save his— Where is the king now?
THOM	Boulogne.
KATE	And wasn't the siege in place before he even got there?
THOM	Yes, / but
KATE	Has he even captured Boulogne yet?
THOM	No . . .

KATE	And you're on your way to help him because he's easily distracted. He's a lousy soldier.
MARY	Wow.
THOM	Respectfully, Your Majesty . . . that remark could be—
MARY	Lesson Three: Denounce the Opposition—
KATE	WILL YOU SHUT UP, MARY!
	(a fact) He needs all the help he can get! You know it. The Council knows it.
THOM	You're going too far.
KATE	I can't go far enough. Not when it comes to the welfare of England.
THOM	*(says nothing)*
KATE	So. Tell the Council to draft a letter to His Majesty telling him that the rumours of an enemy landing off the coast were monstrously inflated, that he should focus on capturing Boulogne, and not worry in the slightest about security here. Bring the king home, Thom.
THOM	*(catching her)* Sir Thomas.
KATE	Sorry?
MARY	Bring the king home . . . Sir Thomas.
KATE	I meant—
	THOM goes to leave. KATE follows him.
THOM	You're sure I can't help.
KATE	I'm doing fine. Mary's just— Am I not doing fine?
THOM	The Council's watching you.
KATE	No wonder I can't get anything done.
THOM	Just don't— I am happy to help.

KATE	I know. But I'm good right here on the edge, thanks.
	KATE goes back to the table. THOM looks at her for a moment, then goes to leave.
BESS	See you, Thom.
THOM	See you, Bess.
MARY	Our greetings to the king.
THOM	I'll be certain to convey them.
	(to KATE) Your Majesty.
	THOM goes. KATE sits with her head in her hands.
BESS	Maybe this is what we need: a roll-on–roll-off cargo ship.
KATE	What's the maximum freight load?
	BESS points to a statistic in the book.
BESS	They call it a ro-ro. Heh heh. Cute.
	KATE kisses BESS.
KATE	Thank God for you, Bess! Mary, start the letters.
MARY	Oh. Is that you asking for my help?
KATE	*Please.* Obtain a voluntary agreement with any merchant who has a—ro-ro—to ship the shovels, the axes, the cannons, and the lead shot.

SCENE SEVENTEEN: THE RETURN OF THE KING

At table. KATE and EDDIE are playing chess.

KATE	Don't you want to counter me?
EDDIE	Nope.
KATE	Sure?

EDDIE	Yup.
KATE	Has Bess been teaching you a new strategy?
EDDIE	Nope.
KATE	Okay. c4.
EDDIE	Yes! g6.
KATE	You're letting me take the centre.
EDDIE	Uhuh.
KATE	You know you want to control the centre.
EDDIE	That's what you taught me.
KATE	Okay. Knight to c3.
EDDIE	Yeah, yeah, yeah!
KATE	What're you doing?
EDDIE	Tricking you.
KATE	I think you're trying to lose.
EDDIE	Keep playing.
KATE	It's your move.
EDDIE	Right. Um. Bishop to g7.
KATE	You're not coming out.
EDDIE	I know.
KATE	You little devil; what have you learned?
EDDIE	Secrets.
KATE	So you can win?
EDDIE	You look very pretty today.
KATE	You look like a little rat.
EDDIE	Play.

KATE   Okay . . .

> *She moves.*

EDDIE   Hah, hah.

> *He moves.*

KATE   Hey. Who taught you this?

EDDIE   Mary.

KATE   Mary. Taught you this opening?

EDDIE   Nope. She said I should make up my own opening.

KATE   In chess? That's her advice? You shouldn't listen to Mary.

EDDIE   She said it was risky but I would learn a lot more making things up than I would doing what everyone has done before.

Play.

KATE   Little bugger.

> *She moves.*

> *EDDIE moves.*

See. I can take you.

EDDIE   It's okay.

KATE   You gave up control of the board.

EDDIE   It's okay.

KATE   It isn't. Why is it okay?

EDDIE   Because I got what I wanted.

KATE   You wanted me to win?

EDDIE   I wanted you to play.

> *HENRY enters.*

HENRY   Why is it the king / can

EDDIE jumps into HENRY's arms.

EDDIE / Daddeeeeee!

HENRY only move one square at a time, when the queen can do whatever she wants? *(over EDDIE's shoulder)* Hello, Mother.

       HENRY winces.

Maybe it's because his leg hurts, poor little king.

EDDIE Sorry.

HENRY It's okay. *(squeezing EDDIE)* Rrrrrr.

EDDIE Did you bring me a present?

HENRY How about this?

       HENRY gives EDDIE a helmet.

EDDIE Is it real?

HENRY "Is it real?" . . . and the chariot.

EDDIE You brought me a chariot?

HENRY With four horses. Go on! Have a look!

       EDDIE runs from the room.

EDDIE Really?! *(as he goes)* I shall be Diocles and you shall be Scorpus! Let's go!

HENRY *(after him)* Can I say hello to Parr?

EDDIE *(from off)* But I'm gonna start without you.

KATE *(after him)* Edward! Don't get too excited . . . it's almost bedtime.

       A moment.

HENRY Greetings.

KATE You look a little wrecked. Sit. Let me take that.

How was your report to Council.

HENRY	Brief.
KATE	Good.
HENRY	I'm a bit old to be a charioteer.
KATE	Ah.

A moment.

HENRY	You saved my ass you know.
KATE	Did I?
HENRY	Getting the ammunition shipped? The old farts on the Council were stunned. And those ridiculous cannons? You're one smart little cookie.
KATE	You know that's derogatory.
HENRY	Old farts? Oh, ridiculous cannons.
KATE	Right.
HENRY	What, smart cookie? Nah. It just means I want to eat you.

HENRY nibbles at KATE.

	So . . . Thomas stopped by before he joined me in France.
KATE	Who told you that?
HENRY	Did he?
KATE	Yes. How do you know?
HENRY	Mary.
KATE	Mary.
HENRY	Did you give him a piece?
KATE	Henry . . .
HENRY	I have a little understanding of that family that you don't. Trust me.
KATE	*Trust* you?

HENRY	He's liming your bush.
KATE	He was paying his regent an official visit.
HENRY	While I was off on the hunt. The smell of another man's urine on the seat. Pungent.

KATE refuses to be stirred.

	You know . . . cookie . . . I'd have to say you, uh, you had some good ideas while I was gone . . . did a pretty fine job as regent.
KATE	I . . . Sorry?—misheard—fine what?
HENRY	Parr . . .
KATE	Flattery's not your style.
HENRY	In the old days, this was called "making love." The Germans were right about the other stuff: we're animals: we fuck. Making love is gratifying in a different way.
KATE	You want to make love to me?
HENRY	I am making love to you. I'm stimulating your mind. Disarming you. Appealing to you. I might start quoting Rumi at any turn.
KATE	And you think I'm falling for this?
HENRY	I'm grateful. You let me go to France and prove my . . . man-thing.
KATE	And how was the . . . man-thing?
HENRY	Well, considering that last week we didn't even have the town . . .
KATE	Then how'd you get back here so fast?

Suddenly animated, HENRY uses the chessboard to demonstrate.

HENRY	Ha, ha! It was so great! Here: so we've taken the castle, and the embankment, and it doesn't look like the French can

take it back; but we're struggling to get a firm hold on the town, right? We have three battalions attacking, and three gunnery squadrons backing them up, but still: deadlock. Then—*finally*—your ridiculous cannons arrive—ta da!—and BOOM! we ripped a great gash out of their most fortified defence wall. That was—well—let's just say the fat lady sang.

KATE laughs.

Not bad for an old buck.

KATE   Not bad at all.

HENRY puts the chessboard aside.

HENRY   So. The Crocodiles. Did they behave for you?

KATE   They sent a lot of couriers. So they wouldn't have to look me in the eye. But they were a cakewalk next to the letters! Good Lord: there must be a hundred every morning!

HENRY   At / least.

KATE   Signing, sealing, signing, sealing . . .

HENRY   Oh, so I'll have to take a look at that proclamation.

KATE gives HENRY a look.

Not now. In the morning. Just to make / sure

KATE   Four. Four proclamations. Actually.

HENRY   Four? Really?

KATE   The girls helped.

HENRY   You had little governing sessions with them did you? Over your tatting?

KATE   I'm not going to bite.

HENRY   And Edward? He got right in there?

KATE   Eddie . . . sure. The girls had more time.

| HENRY | Why not Eddie? |
| KATE | School. That's all. |

A moment.

KATE	What. Henry.
HENRY	Eddie.
	Hnh.
	He's all I have of . . .

A moment.

| KATE | Jane. |

HENRY looks at KATE.

HENRY	Of me. This little runt of a kid. How did that happen?
KATE	He doesn't have to be strong. Surround him with people who are strong.
HENRY	I do— I mean . . . I have.

A moment.

KATE	Hnh. What happened to you in France?
HENRY	I missed you.
KATE	You missed me.

HENRY reaches tentatively for KATE's hand.

HENRY	Happy?
KATE	Certainly content.
HENRY	Wanna make happy?
KATE	You're tired.
HENRY	It's up to you.

KATE leads HENRY to the bed.

HENRY   My damn leg . . .

KATE   Feel . . . here . . . how soft.

HENRY   Oh. That helps.

KATE   Kiss me.

He does.

Be kind, Hal.

I don't need virility.

HENRY   I don't know anything about kindness, Parr.

KATE   You've only chosen to forget.

KATE gently touches HENRY. HENRY stops her for a moment.

HENRY   Am I rotting from the inside out?

* * *

In private. EDDIE wakes from a dream, obviously frightened.

EDDIE   Mommy!

* * *

At bed. HENRY is sleeping. KATE is sitting up.

KATE   Hal?

HENRY   Yuh.

KATE   You awake?

HENRY   No.

KATE   Can I talk to you?

HENRY	No.
KATE	Shut up.
HENRY	Okay.
KATE	I . . . Are you listening?

HENRY rolls over.

HENRY	Yes.

A moment.

And then she said nothing.

KATE	No, it's— I was just thinking about . . . Before you left . . .

A moment.

HENRY	Take your time.
KATE	Well, things were—weren't things good here? Between us?
HENRY	Uhuh.
KATE	And then . . . I don't know . . . It was really brave of you to make me regent; I just want to say that.
HENRY	I'm a brave kinda guy.
KATE	To let me protect Eddie, it . . . it just felt . . . well, it gave me confidence, to get your approval, you know?
HENRY	Yuh.
KATE	I mean, to work so hard for the good of the country. To succeed at that. It's . . . just . . . great, Hal.
HENRY	Good.
KATE	And you.

She kisses him, plays with his hair.

France was good for you.

She smiles. Deeply satisfied.

I feel fierce. And a bit . . . giddy.

Thank you.

HENRY   You couldn't be more welcome.

KATE   I'm sure looking forward to more.

HENRY   I'm looking forward to less. Enough Diocles and Scopus for me.

KATE   Well, you can count on having some help here.

HENRY   With what?

KATE   I mean, I can take some of the audiences off your plate for starters, deal with half the signing and sealing . . .

HENRY props himself up.

Whatever works for you, really. We'll look at it in the morning when you check the proclamations. See how we move forward together.

KATE lies back down.

HENRY   Together.

HENRY is now sitting up and very alert. KATE leans in to cuddle HENRY.

KATE   Perfectly together.

HENRY   Sharing responsibility. Authority.

KATE   *(playful)* I like it on top.

HENRY stops her hand.

HENRY   *(dangerous)* Don't.

A moment.

KATE   Don't wh-what?

HENRY   Don't think that—

A moment.

KATE   Think. What. Did I say something / that

> *HENRY gets out of bed.*

HENRY   Not. One. Goddamned Person.

KATE   What have I said— Henry? Don't be so—

HENRY   WHAT?! CHILDISH?!

KATE   Where are you going?

> *As he leaves, not looking back:*

HENRY   Let's be very clear, Katherine: When I went to France, I left a kitten to distract the FUCKING WOLVES!!

SCENE EIGHTEEN: POWER SWITCH

> *In private. KATE and MARY. MARY is not well. KATE opens her little wooden box, takes out a stone and some herbs.*

KATE   Take this. Put it under your tongue.

MARY   It's a rock.

KATE   It's clean. Just do it.

MARY   Are you a witch?

KATE   Because I know things you don't know?

MARY   Yeah.

KATE   Suck on the stone, will you.

> *MARY puts the stone under her tongue.*

I need your help.

MARY   You? Need me?

KATE	What grounds does your father need to kill a wife?
MARY	Whoa—what? Has he threatened you?
KATE	Not yet.
MARY	He doesn't really need grounds. He can just make shit up.
KATE	But in his own mind. What is it that turns the tide.

MARY *takes the stone out of her mouth.*

MARY	What happened?
KATE	I'm not sure; that's what I'm afraid of.
MARY	Did you threaten him?
KATE	No. With what? How could I threaten him?
MARY	By being right; by taking charge; being strong.
KATE	Oh he made it quite clear which one of us is strong.
MARY	Not him.
KATE	Not him?
MARY	He's not strong.
KATE	Henry the Eighth?
MARY	Strong people don't have to drive. They can look out at the horizon and appreciate the scenery because they feel safe. Henry hasn't watched the trees go by since he was a kid. He can only white-knuckle it; he can only keep his eyes fixed on the road. And if someone cuts him off, he doesn't swerve: no, he flattens them like a pancake.
KATE	Oh boy.
MARY	Did you cut him off?
KATE	I blindsided him.
MARY	Great.

KATE	I only turned my head for a second, and—
MARY	Splat.
	Well.
	Here we go again!
KATE	Thanks for understanding!
MARY	How many times do you think we want to get thrown to the dogs because another one of his wives has smoked it.
KATE	You're not being thrown to the dogs. I can turn him around. I talked myself into this mess; I can just as easily talk myself out again. I'll reason with him, clarify my position; he'll see. He's a smart man. He married me because I'm a smart woman. He appreciates / my forthrightness
MARY	Stop! Your brain won't help you now.
KATE	Then what will?
MARY	You won't like it.
KATE	Don't toy with me. Help me!
MARY	Be more like Jane.
KATE	Jane? No. That isn't what he wants? I've got a lot more going on than Jane.
MARY	*(as if being attacked)* The dogs!! The dogs!!
KATE	Okayyy. What.
MARY	She had a few tricks up her sleeve, did pretty little Jane. If I were you, I'd learn to thread a needle.
KATE	You think embroidery will win him back?
MARY	I think sex will win him back. But embroidery's pretty good foreplay.

SCENE NINETEEN: DEFENDING THE FAITH

In private. HENRY *is embroidering.* KATE *is in defence-attorney mode.*

HENRY   What do you want?

KATE   I want to talk to you.

HENRY   I'm busy.

KATE   I see that.

HENRY   *(says nothing)*

KATE   I want to know why you aren't sharing my bed. Why you won't take meals with me. I want to know what happens next.

HENRY   *(says nothing)*

KATE   So, no discussion. No opportunity to mount a defence. No right to face my accuser, to hear the charges against / me

HENRY   I'm your accuser. Face away.

KATE   Well then?

HENRY   Heresy and treason. Same old, same old.

KATE   Completely unfounded.

HENRY   Not this time. Not. Actually.

KATE   What could possibly be the justification that you've trumped up?

HENRY   Witchcraft. Blasphemy.

KATE   Witchcraft?

HENRY   If you're not a witch, why are you so good at healing my leg?

KATE   You're accusing me of heresy because I make you feel better?

HENRY	Did you learn it from your mother? Why didn't she marry again when your father died?
KATE	She was content being alone.
HENRY	They say you use sorcery to keep from getting pregnant.
KATE	They—? You think I don't want to have a child with you?
HENRY	Why do you keep heretical books in your library?
KATE	Heret— I keep books about the Reformation in my library. My husband, Henry, the King of England, France, and Ireland, reformed the church, remember?
HENRY	Don't, DON'T try to teach me like I'm one of the CHILDREN! I'm not just abandoning my lifelong beliefs because you and your liberal pals think they're out of fashion!
KATE	Let me get this straight: you're accusing me of witchcraft because I'm a good doctor, and treason because I'm a good teacher.
HENRY	This is not a GAME! Have you not seen what happens, time and again, when people try to convince me that things should just be done their way? You're mad to think they won't kill you for that.
KATE	That *who* won't kill me? Who is in this room, Henry, besides you and me? It's not my ambition that's got you riled up! I've cut somewhere way closer to the quick, haven't I?
HENRY	*(sharply)* You and I have a contract. Don't think it's anything else.
KATE	This is *love*! This right now. This yelling? This . . . *exasperation*? This is *trust*. This is me being the mother to your children. This is you accepting that you have shame and fear, and that I have shame and fear, and that you have a heart, and I have a brain. This is a real partnership! You LOVE me. I LOVE

you. Whether we like it or not. Whether it's convenient or not. This is more than you ever had with Jane—

HENRY   Don't / you

KATE   she couldn't even read!

HENRY   Oh / boy

KATE   How could she possibly be your equal?! She's lucky she died giving birth to Eddie. How long would it have been before you got totally bored with her, like you did with that Howard twit? How long / till you

HENRY   / Kate . . .

KATE   would have cut off her

> HENRY *slaps* KATE *hard across the face.*

Hal . . .

> KATE *staggers.*

Oh God.

HENRY   Is this what you want?! Is this what you think I want?!

> HENRY *takes the ring from* KATE's *finger, crushes it beneath his foot.*

KATE   Get your hands off me!

HENRY   Damn you!

KATE   Damn *me*?! Why?! I should be damned because you can't accept what I am?! Or are you going to say I asked for it.

> HENRY *raises his fist. A stunned moment.* HENRY *struggles.* KATE's *world stops.* KATE *drops to her knees.* HENRY *reaches for* KATE. *She flinches.*

HENRY   Oh God.

> HENRY *goes.* KATE *pleads for her life as she picks up the pieces of her ring.*

KATE O Thou Lord, Thou only art our King. Help me, desolate woman, which have no helper but Thee, for my misery and destruction is hard at my hand.

I have sinned above the number of sands of the sea and there is in me no breathing. I have provoked Thine anger. And now I bow the knees of my heart, requiring goodness of Thee, O Lord. I have sinned, Lord; I have sinned, and know my iniquity. O Lord: forgive me, forgive me, and destroy me not along with mine iniquities. But save me by Thy great mercy, and I will praise Thee everlastingly all the days of my life.

THOM comes around the corner, sees KATE.

THOM What happened—here—Good Lord—what's—? Let me help you. Here.

KATE looks at THOM but has no words.

You're flushed. Hey . . . *(her tears)* Are you hurt?

KATE Help me. Help me.

THOM I could kill / that bastard

KATE I'm scared. I can't do it on / my own.

THOM I'm here. Here. Okay now. You're safe with me.

He dries her tears, smooths her hair.

* * *

In private. HENRY and MARY.

MARY She was nice to us! She was nice to you! Just because she's a bit of a challenge doesn't mean you should chop off her head! You like her! I know you do!

HENRY Are you trying to cheer me up?

MARY	Come on! Please. Don't fuck this up.
HENRY	*(adamant)* She's no Jane.
MARY	Did I say she was?

* * *

In private. KATE and THOM.

KATE	Heresy and treason. He says he has proof.
THOM	If he doesn't, he'll find it. He has the means.
KATE	What, torture? Me?
THOM	Your friends. In the tower. As we speak.
KATE	You're serious?
THOM	Others do his dirty work. That leaves him time to toy with us.
KATE	What do you mean?
THOM	Why else would he bring me here?

> *He figures it out.*

To deliver the warrant.

> *KATE's legs give way.*

* * *

In private. MARY and HENRY.

HENRY	Mary.
MARY	What.
HENRY	You're right to blame me. For what you are.

MARY   I don't. Not that I forgive you. But, in a way that . . . kinda makes me wanna barf just a bit . . . I understand you.

HENRY   Will you promise me something? I need you to promise me something.

MARY   What?

HENRY   It's to do with Thom.

MARY   If I promise, will you go to her?

HENRY   What good will it do.

MARY   Don't look at me. Figure it out!

* * *

In private. KATE *and* THOM.

KATE   I don't know what to do. I don't know what I should do.

        A moment.

        Thom . . .

        A moment.

        What would Jane do?

THOM   Jane . . . would . . . use the sex.

KATE   Would she? Really? As a bargain for her life?!

THOM   You'd rather something more noble? There's a warrant for your arrest!

KATE   Use my body!

THOM   I'm not . . . It can't be that big a deal.

KATE   Can't be . . . ? Oh. You want me to do that. You're asking me to / do

THOM   I'm not asking you to— It's a pretty easy way to stay alive!

SCENE TWENTY: THREADING THE NEEDLE

At bed. KATE is sitting on the edge of the bed. HENRY enters.
He sits on a chair.

KATE   I heard.

HENRY   Heard what?

KATE   The warrant. You want me dead.

HENRY   *(says nothing)*

KATE   Hal.

   A moment.

   Hal.

HENRY   I'm stuck here.

KATE   I see that.

HENRY   I can't brook dissension.

KATE   Right.

HENRY   If I can't control my own household, how can I possibly control a whole country?

KATE   Can we go back? To when you came in with the helmet?

HENRY   What do you think.

KATE   I'll say what's necessary. I'll say what you need me to say.

HENRY   I want you to understand why I'm right!

KATE   I do. I will.

HENRY   Not to mollify me, damn it! In your heart!

KATE   You and I both know the imperfection and weakness of women: created and appointed as inferior—

HENRY   Shit . . .

KATE	and subject to man as our head; from which head all our direction ought to proceed; by whom she is to be governed, commanded, and directed; her natural faults to be tolerated, aided, and borne, so that by his wisdom things lacking in her might be supplied.
	KATE undoes her dress.
	It has to come from you.
HENRY	No . . .
	She sits on his lap.
KATE	Kiss me.
	He does.
	Again.
	He does.
HENRY	You don't want this . . . Don't do this . . .
KATE	Love me, Hal.
HENRY	I'm a bear
KATE	You are my only anchor.
	She kisses him.
HENRY	I'm lost now; you know I am.
	She kisses him.
	HENRY is lost.
KATE	Can you reverse the warrant?
	I don't want to die.
	She kisses him.
	Reverse the warrant.
	Henry.
	I don't want to die.

SCENE TWENTY-ONE: WHACK-A-MOLE

In private. THOM *has the warrant.* HENRY *is beating* THOM.
KATE *looks on.*

HENRY   How could you idiots / make

THOM   / Majesty!

HENRY   such ludicrous accusations against this woman?!

THOM   The Council was mistaken, / I'm sure.

HENRY   This kind, gentle—you made up the most inane lies about
          her— / give me that

THOM   Careful, Majesty: your / leg

          HENRY *tears up the warrant.*

HENRY   I can't believe I ever signed this stupid thing, that you had
          the balls to deliver / it!

THOM   Yes, sir. I was wrong to

          HENRY *grabs* THOM *by the throat and begins to choke him.*

KATE   Henry! Stop it!

          KATE *pulls* HENRY *off* THOM.

HENRY   *(to* KATE*)* I was going to Have You Killed!

          (to THOM*)* See her?! She can save your miserable little ass
          because she has always loved you. And at the same time she
          can stand by a man whose soul is going straight to hell. That's
          the kind of woman she really is. Now get out of my sight, you
          goddamn weasel.

          THOM *goes.* HENRY, *in pain, goes to the bed.*

SCENE TWENTY-TWO: REPRIEVE

In private. KATE *sits in her nightgown in equal measures of relief and misery.* BESS *enters, carrying a small embroidered book.*

BESS Hi Kate.

KATE Hi Bess.

BESS Can I come in?

KATE Sure.

BESS You okay?

KATE I will be.

BESS You look sad.

KATE It's been a rough few weeks.

BESS For us too.

KATE I'm sorry. I'm afraid I wasn't thinking much of you.

> BESS *holds out the book.*

BESS I brought you a present.

KATE Me?

BESS It's a book.

KATE It's so . . . oh . . . it's . . . breathtaking.

BESS I made it.

KATE It's my prayers and meditations.

BESS I copied them out. Translated them too.

KATE Look at you:

> KATE *carefully turns the pages.*

French . . . Italian . . .

BESS	And Latin. At the back. I thought you'd like the Latin.

KATE holds the book between her hands.

KATE	Do you know what scared me the most? when I knew the warrant was coming?
BESS	What?
KATE	That I would die without having children.
BESS	But . . . ? No.
KATE	What?
BESS	You have three.
KATE	Yes . . .
BESS	Do you know what scared me?
KATE	What?
BESS	That you would leave me your purple dress.

SCENE TWENTY-THREE: IMPOTENCE

At bed. HENRY sits on one side of the bed. KATE sits on the other. There is a silence filled with awkward disbelief and physical inaction.

HENRY	I
KATE	/ I

—you go.

HENRY	No, it's . . .

Nothing.

I can't . . .

KATE	Yes.

HENRY	I can't . . .
KATE	We don't have to.
HENRY	We—
KATE	It's okay.
HENRY	Sorry.
KATE	No, I'm—

Nothing.

Just being together / is

HENRY	What, you just want to cuddle with the old, smelly, fat guy?
KATE	I . . . I'm h-happy. With that.
HENRY	Are you my mother, now?
KATE	You're not well.
HENRY	Don't tell me that!
KATE	We'll try again later, when you're . . .
HENRY	Younger?

Nothing.

I want to quit seeing you. I'm going to quit seeing you.

KATE	Seeing me?
HENRY	I can't fuck you anymore!
KATE	Okay, now just / stop this
HENRY	There's no point in you being around. I have doctors to take care of me. It won't be much longer.
KATE	You can't. just. cut me out like that.
HENRY	Are you telling me what I can do?
KATE	Of course not. I'll do what you say. You do what you like.

HENRY	You creep around me now.
KATE	You threatened to kill me!
HENRY	I know what I did! You don't have to tell me. I know what I've done!
KATE	Sorry.
HENRY	Don't—!

In silence, HENRY moves to KATE. HENRY touches KATE's face carefully, as if she might shatter. Then slowly attempts:

You see with Jane . . .

You are so much . . .

Teach my son, Kate. Teach Bess. Something other than this.

HENRY holds Kate's hand. Then he stands; he moves away.

I'm gonna be buried beside Jane.

KATE	Oh.
HENRY	Sorry.

You'll have Christmas at Greenwich with the children.

I'm going to London alone.

KATE	No— Wait.

With the children?

HENRY	Edward too.
KATE	You want me to care for Eddie?
HENRY	It's all in my will. You'll head a sixteen-man Council.
KATE	/ I'll
HENRY	You'll have no veto, no extraordinary powers, just a vote: one vote, like all the others. But you'll be Protector. There's no one better suited to that title.

SCENE TWENTY-FOUR: GOOD COUNCIL

> *In public.* KATE, MARY, *and* BESS *are in front of the door to* HENRY's *rooms. For a time they sit in silence.*

BESS   / But why won't he—?

MARY   How long do we—?

> *More silence.*

We've been waiting here three days in a row. What can they possibly be doing in there?

KATE   He'll see us, it's just . . . Bureaucracy . . . takes time.

> *More silence.* THOM *enters from* HENRY's *rooms.*

THOM   The king doesn't want any women to witness his passing. I tried.

KATE   He doesn't—what? No. I'm supposed to—

THOM   The Council voted / and

KATE   The Council voted? That's—

> KATE *tries to get past* THOM.

No. I'm supposed to be in there.

> THOM *stops her.*

Thom?

THOM   I have no choice.

KATE   I have a vote. I was given a vote!

THOM   The king sent you this.

> THOM *hands* KATE *a note.*

I'm sorry.

KATE reads the note. She's paralyzed. She drops the note. BESS picks it up. Reads:

BESS   "Too much at stake."

MARY   Hah! When will there not be?!

THOM   You can communicate with Edward through letters from time to / time.

KATE   No, no, / no.

THOM   I know.

KATE   They can't take / Eddie!

THOM   The Council feels that they can best provide for Edward's / future.

KATE   He's. My. Son.

THOM   He's Jane's son.

KATE walks away. More silence. KATE rallies.

KATE   But Henry was clear—

MARY   Oath schmoath.

KATE   He was very clear about what should become of the children.

THOM   You can't just flip the entire system on its head. You need a realistic plan.

This stops KATE in her tracks.

KATE   Wh-what?

THOM   You can't just flip the entire system on its head. You have to follow the rules. Just like we do.

This lands hard on KATE.

KATE   And who got to make those rules in the first place.

BESS   Can we really not see him?

KATE   The loyalty of love means nothing here.

This lands hard on THOM.

MARY   Darn. I would've liked to say I saw him die.

Come on, little girl.

BESS   See you, Thom.

THOM   See you, Bess.

       MARY and BESS *go.* KATE *and* THOM *stay. A silence.*

The loyalty of love.

KATE   I AM HIS PROTECTOR!!!

       A moment.

THOM   I really am sorry.

       A moment.

KATE   Did he give you a title?

THOM   Lord High Admiral. And First Earl of Sudeley.

       KATE *laughs or cries or both.*

KATE   How did we get here?

THOM   How do we ever get back?

SCENE TWENTY-FIVE: KING EDWARD VI'S LATIN LETTER TO DOWAGER QUEEN KATHERINE

      In private. EDDIE *reads aloud the letter he has written to his mother.*

EDDIE   To Queen Katherine,

Many thanks to you for the last letter that you sent me, dearest mother, which certainly is a mark of your daily love for me.

Furthermore, that it has seemed good that my father and your husband, the most illustrious King, should end this life, it is a grief common to us both together.

Although nature commands us, even so, to grieve and pour out tears for the departure of him who is absent, yet prudence commands us to moderate those feelings. Besides, since Your Highness has bestowed so many kindnesses on me, I ought to offer whatever comfort I can bring you. I wish Your Highness great good health. Farewell, dearest mother.

EDDIE makes a correction.

Farewell, revered Queen.

He signs the letter.

Edward . . . the . . . King.

SCENE TWENTY-SIX: A LITTLE PLEASURE

At bed. KATE *and* THOM *lie flat on their backs beside each other . . . quite possibly panting.*

THOM   Good Lord.

They both laugh like teenagers. It is a release of the last three years.

I love you?

KATE   I know.

THOM   Okay.

KATE ponders the transition from HENRY *to what comes after* HENRY.

KATE   I can't seem to put one foot in front of the other.

THOM   You will. I think . . . you . . . will.

KATE	This is what's next. I get that. I want—I think I—no, I know I want this; I've always—

KATE turns to look at THOM.

	It's nearly seven.
THOM	Right.

THOM gets up to go. KATE turns around.

KATE	Hey.
THOM	Yup.
KATE	That was fun.
THOM	Told ya.

THOM goes. KATE, still on the bed, doesn't move.

SCENE TWENTY-SEVEN: BURN THE PLAYHOUSE DOWN

In public. Over a year later. MARY, who has not been well, sits alone. THOM and BESS enter. BESS stops upon seeing MARY.

BESS	Oh! When did you get here?
MARY	Or: "Beautiful sister: I understand you've been under the weather, yet your cheerful presence suggests that the worst is finally over."
BESS	Hi Mary.
THOM	Hi Mary.
MARY	How was riding?
BESS	We jumped.
MARY	How high?

BESS	Thomas showed me: you just have to lean in, squeeze your legs, and pick the horse up with you! Then over you go! It's really cool.
THOM	She's a natural.
MARY	She's impressionable.

KATE enters with her healing box. She is six months pregnant.

KATE	You're back. How was riding?
BESS	We jumped.
KATE	You jumped?
THOM	Have you been sitting at all?
KATE	Stop nagging me.
THOM	I'm taking care of my little mouse.

THOM touches KATE's belly.

In his little house.

MARY looks away.

MARY	*(sharply)* Don't—

MARY paces in agitation.

THOM	*(stung)* Don't what?
MARY	*(to KATE)* Sit down.
KATE	Really?
MARY	Yes!

KATE sits.

Okay. So. Before Henry died—when you and he were in the worst of it, remember?—I made him a promise that once his dust had settled I'd keep my eye on the old Seymour clan.

KATE	Honestly, / Mary

MARY	No, look. I went along with your marriage to Thomas, and even the baby thing, because, well, there was no danger and I knew how happy it made you, Kate; I do, but— Yesterday, in town, I heard a rumour about Bess . . . a dangerous rumour, / one that
KATE	Dangerous?
MARY	could threaten the safety of the second in line to the throne, and it reminded me of—well, of your title. And that a promise is a promise.
KATE	My title?
MARY	*(to THOM)* It's about your morning visits to Bess's bedroom before she's dressed.
BESS	/ Mary!
THOM	What?!
MARY	About the governess seeing you in each other's arms.
KATE	He goes there to wake her up. What's so dangerous about that?
MARY	Do you go with him?
KATE	*(no)* He's her stepfather.
MARY	Well, he sort of is that; he's sort of her uncle; he's sort of her cousin, but he's definitely a Seymour.
	There's more. A piece of information that Henry would want you to have. *(looking at THOM)* Bess: Tell Kate about the letter you got from Thom after father died.
	BESS is paralyzed.
BESS	The letter? How do you / know . . . ?
THOM	Mary. Mary, what are you trying / to do?
MARY	Do your duty, Bess. This is bigger than you or Kate.
BESS	*(trying to keep her secret)* Mary. / Don't.

KATE	What letter, Bess?
THOM	*(to KATE)* This isn't what it looks like. / I
KATE	It doesn't look like anything.
MARY	I got one too.
BESS	You never did.
	(to THOM) She never did.
THOM	*(to MARY)* Stop this.
	(to KATE) Kate, really, stop this.
BESS	You're just doing this because you hate me.
MARY	I certainly didn't take mine seriously.
KATE	What was in the letter, Bess?
THOM	It's a misunder/standing.
KATE	Then Bess can tell me.
BESS	But / Thom, you
KATE	/ Tell me!
MARY	Tell her!
BESS	You said my skin was beautiful. That I was Henry's true heir. That you would be a great match for me, our families / and all.
THOM	Stop talking, / Bess.
KATE	Don't bully / her.
THOM	I'm not, I— Let me ex/plain—
BESS	That you wanted to marry a princess.
KATE	You said / that?
THOM	The whole court was jockeying for position.
KATE	When did you send these letters?

MARY	Father had just died.
THOM	Before we got back together!
KATE	I was grieving the loss of my / husband.
BESS	But you've always been so / nice to me.
THOM	*(to KATE)* Exactly. Neither of us knew how to—I just didn't know what we / had!
BESS	And so good- / looking.
KATE	*(to THOM)* We *had* . . . to wait! We *had* . . . something to look forward to!
THOM	No, you *had*. You *had* a king. You *had* a country. I was nothing next to what you *had*.
MARY	He was pissed off that you didn't get Eddie. That's what he's wanted all / along.
THOM	That's not / true!
BESS	And such a good / dancer.
MARY	That'd make you the power couple. The bigger snag would be if Kate's carrying Henry's boy.
KATE	Don't / be
MARY	That'd throw everyone into a tizzy.
THOM	That's *MY* boy. That, *THAT* is something Henry could never do.
KATE	You are kidding me: I'm pregnant with your child so . . . you're a bigger man than Henry because your seed took?
THOM	No. Don't, I— I love you. Please don't. I just. Oh God. I thought you loved him.
KATE	I did.
THOM	You confuse me. I'm trying to— Look, Bess and I— Bess. No. You and I, right? We are. We always have been. Something . . . right? Something good.

KATE	Inexplicably.
THOM	Please don't drop it. Okay?
KATE	She's a child living in our house.
THOM	I was tickling her, that's all. That's what the governess saw. That's *all* the governess saw.

KATE feels safe.

KATE	Let me talk to Bess.
THOM	Okay.

THOM touches BESS.

This is the new. This is the start. Again.

THOM leaves. There is silence while BESS and MARY look at KATE.

MARY	Don't trust him.
KATE	I do. You can't change that.
MARY	It's your life.

(KATE's belly) How does it feel? That. Getting bigger and bigger.

I'd like to have a kid, but I worry about that. How big.

(making an icky face) Ew.

MARY finds KATE's little wooden box, takes a stone out, puts it in her mouth, and sits. KATE turns to BESS.

BESS	I do take after my mother, don't I. / Don't I!
KATE	Nothing you do is private. Nothing. Mary's right. We have to protect you.
BESS	Ohh, now I'm scared. Because when I do things wrong, I . . .

KATE searches for a way to move forward.

I know what you're going to say. Just say it.

KATE   You have to go away from / here

BESS   Noooo! / See!

KATE   Just for a while. It's not a punish/ment

BESS   You hate me! This is what happens. You both hate / me!

KATE   Bess: the Council will grab that rumour and ruin you. They'll take what's yours by right—by law—because they can't kill you. We have to protect who you are; how people see you.

BESS   But I'm not— Thom's / not

KATE   It doesn't matter what's true about Thom. You have to take what happened here and make it clean. Make it good. Make yourself innocent. I will. Mary will.

MARY   Me . . . ?

KATE   Go to Hatfield. You'll be safe. We'll all be safe.

BESS   I'll be helping you? If I go?

KATE   And yourself.

BESS   And Thom?

KATE puts her arms around BESS.

KATE   And Thom.

BESS   Can I still call you Mother?

KATE takes BESS's hand and puts it on her belly.

KATE   Always.

BESS smiles.

BESS   Have you picked out a name?

KATE   Mary.

MARY spits out the stone.

EPILOGUE: QUEENMAKER

In private. Five years later. At Katherine Parr's sepulchre. BESS *holds a pile of books.* MARY *holds* KATE's *little wooden box, and a note.*

BESS   What's the note?

MARY   A shipping label:

"Parcel of the Queen's jewels and other stuff, which come from the late Admiral's house of Sudeley, in the county of Gloucestershire."

BESS   Poor Thom.

MARY   After what he did to you, you still—? If Eddie hadn't killed him, I'd have done it myself. *She's* the one who should have lived.

BESS   No one is innocent.

MARY   What happened between you and Thom—well, it didn't change the way she thought of you.

A moment.

BESS   You don't mind doing this?

MARY   She was the only mother you had. And she was my friend. Even if we had our differences.

BESS   And our differences?

MARY   This we share.

BESS   Okay.

MARY   So. Do we have it all?

BESS   I have all the books.

MARY   Then you start.

BESS organizes herself and looks heavenward. She holds up
each of the books as she names them.

BESS Hi Mother: Bess here. We wanted to commemorate you
somehow. We know how sad you'd be that Eddie died. But
at least you saw him on the throne. And anyway, I wanted
to get all your books into one place, so . . . Here they are:
your books; first the ones you wrote. And . . . also, the book
I gave you for the New Year that time, and here, your second
husband's Bible.

A legacy. Never to be disregarded.

Your Highness's humble daughter, Elizabeth.

MARY lifts the objects from the box as she names them.

MARY Mother. Katherine. Kate: Thomas and Ted are both dead,
and I got your stuff back from their nasty family. A promise
to Father.

Your box of stones from the North; your mother's pearl; the
little picture you gave Eddie; a piece of unicorn's horn; and
the two broken parts of your ring, with a spark of a ruby.
From Henry. You were nothing like my real mother, but you
did your best.

Your most humble daughter and servant, Mary.

MARY looks at BESS. A moment.

You have the hair.

BESS Shoot. I forgot.

BESS takes a lock of baby hair from her pocket.

From your third daughter, little Mary Seymour, the child of
your flesh.

A moment.

MARY Okay.

BESS   Let's hold hands.

MARY   Really?

> BESS *and* MARY, *holding hands, read an epitaph that they have prepared.*

BESS &
MARY   "In this urn lies Katherine:
Lately Queen of England,
Women's greatest glory.
She died in giving birth.
After bringing forth an infant girl,
Lo, at daylight's seventh shining,
She breathed her spirit forth."

> BESS *and* MARY *stand looking straight ahead.*

BESS   Okay.

MARY   Okay.

BESS   I'm glad we did this.

MARY   Yup.

> *A silence.* BESS *looks at* MARY.

BESS   What will we do now, Mary?

> MARY *marches off.*

MARY   *(as she goes)* We'll make history!

> BESS *is left alone.*

APPENDIX

Katherine Parr died of puerperal fever on September 5, 1548. She was the first woman to publish her own writing, under her own name, in the English language. She was an avid religious reformist, a patroness of arts and education, and a lover of fabulous clothes. Her motto was: "To be useful in all I do."

Thomas Seymour was tried on thirty-three counts of treason. Elizabeth was questioned as a possible co-conspiritor during his trial. She was exonerated.He was found guilty and was executed on March 20, 1549. His sentence was signed by his nephew, Edward VI.

Mary Seymour became the ward of Catherine Brandon (a friend of Katherine Parr's) after the execution of Thomas Seymour. Her death was never recorded, but documents of her life cease to exist much past her second birthday in 1550.

Henry VIII reigned from 1509 to his death on January 28, 1547. He was a poet, a songwriter/musician, and was purported to have enjoyed needlework. The wound on his leg may have been caused by garters that he wore to show off his calves.

Edward VI reigned from 1547 until his death on July 6, 1553. He was nine years old when he became king. He left Lady Jane Grey as his heir, attempting to disinherit his sisters, Mary and Elizabeth.

Mary I (Bloody Mary) was the first reigning Queen of England, from 1553 to her death of influenza on November 17, 1558. She married Philip II of Spain to secure land and riches for England and to beget a Catholic heir. She had two false pregnancies (possibly cysts or uterine cancer) and left the kingdom to her sister, Elizabeth. Her motto was: "Truth is the daughter of Time."

Elizabeth I (The Virgin Queen; Gloriana; Good Queen Bess) reigned from 1558 until her death on March 24, 1603. She was moderate, tolerant, perhaps indecisive, and a lover of plays. A cult grew up around her virginity in the latter part of her reign. She was the last of the Tudor line. Her motto was: "Always the same."

ACKNOWLEDGEMENTS

The great director/playwright/actor Neil Munro once said to me, as we were working on one of my plays in his living room, "At some point someone just has to take a chance on your writing." I acknowledge Neil for his wisdom and encouragement and the Stratford Festival for taking a chance.

My thanks to the actors who read my developing scripts with such skill, dedication, and enthusiasm: Jenny Young, Diana Donnelly, Claire Lautier, Robert Persichini, Jim Mezon, Tom McCamus, Randy Hughson, Susanna Fournier, Madeline Kennedy, Jacquelyn French, Ijeoma Emesowum, Katie Swift, Tara Rosling, Stacy Smith, Sabryn Rock, Sara Farb, Jordan Pettle, Kevin Hanchard, Tim Campbell, Gareth Potter, Rhys Fulton-Doyle, Jordan Hilliker, Andre Morin, Josh Buchwald, Marvin Ishmael, Graeme Somerville, and Bona Duncan (Stage Manager).

Thanks to Andy McKim and Bob White for full-court dramaturgy along the way. Special thanks to Tanja Jacobs for her dramaturgical and directorial determination, which resulted in the seminal draft. Thanks also to David Campion, Ilana Landsberg-Lewis, Maggie Huculak, David Scammell, Diana Donnelly, Beth Russell, Elizabeth Sheffield, Payton Smith, and Breanna Smith for their assistance and insight; to Kirsty Saul of Sudeley Castle, Mayor Thomas Clare and his attendant

Peter Cannon of the Kendal Town Council, and Hilary Beaton for research assistance; to Theatre Passe Muraille, the Shaw Festival, and the Stratford Festival for facilitation; and to Nightwood Theatre for the OAC Theatre Creators' Reserve recommendation.

Gratitude always to the Gary Goddard Agency who has represented me for thirty years (Celia Chassels and Emma Laird, the best agents in the WORLD!).

Gratitude to the Fates and Janel Mueller for publishing *Katherine Parr: Complete Works and Correspondence* (University of Chicago Press) two months after I began research for this play.

Born in England and raised in Alberta, Kate is a diverse, multi-award-winning theatre artist with over thirty years of professional experience as a performer, including seasons on Broadway, with the Royal Shakespeare Company, and with both the Shaw and Stratford Festivals. She has an MA in Voice Studies from the Central School of Speech and Drama in London, England. As a writer and performer, Kate is drawn to subjects and characters that give women a greater historical content and context for their cultural lives while striving to balance gender perspectives on our stages. Kate is currently writing two companion pieces to *The Last Wife: The Virgin Trial* and *Father's Daughter*. The trilogy is a contemporary feminist imagining of the Tudor queens Katherine Parr, Mary I, and Elizabeth I. Kate's other playwriting includes *The Eleventh David*—based on ninth-century Japanese poetess Ono No Komachi; *Waterworks*—an epic family drama about the infectious nature of lies, set during the flu pandemic of 1918; and *More*—a pre-industrial-age story of the culture of infertility. Kate is Playwright-in-Residence at Theatre Passe Muraille, Toronto. She lives and writes in the Niagara Region of Canada. www.katehennig.com

First edition: August 2015. Second printing: September 2016.
Printed and bound in Canada by Imprimerie Gauvin, Gatineau

Cover photo of *Curtain* © Daniel Arsham

**PLAYWRIGHTS
CANADA PRESS**
202-269 Richmond St. W.
Toronto, ON
M5V 1X1

416.703.0013
info@playwrightscanada.com
playwrightscanada.com

A **bundled** eBook edition is available
with the purchase of this print book.

CLEARLY PRINT YOUR NAME ABOVE IN UPPER CASE

Instructions to claim your eBook edition:
1. Download the BitLit app for Android or iOS
2. Write your name in **UPPER CASE** above
3. Use the BitLit app to submit a photo
4. Download your eBook to any device

MIX
Paper from
responsible sources
FSC® C100212